Late winter snowstorms frost the Sangre de Cristo mountains near Santa Fe as we prepare to send the *New Mexico Treasures: 2024 Engagement Calendar* to press. When the finished product arrives later this summer, neatly packed into boxes and ready to be shipped to locations near and far, those mountains will have shed their snow and will be ringing with thunder, green from summer rain. That's the expectation. And yet, though there is comfort in anticipating the rhythm of the seasons, uncertainty hangs in the air. Enormous fires, a persistent drought, rain coming in deluges—even the familiar patterns of nature are shifting, making it difficult to predict what lies ahead. Snowy peaks and abundant summer rains may become a rare sight for New Mexicans. Still, I'm certain that the love of place shared in the photographs in this calendar will remain, no matter the weather or how our landscapes might change.

This compelling love of place (some of us here in this state call it querencia) has long inspired New Mexicans as well as sojourners from elsewhere. A steady stream of photographers, artists, and writers has tried to express it, and it shines in the people, landscapes, and ever-dazzling skies of New Mexico in the photographs in this calendar—weekly reminders that there is much to love and be grateful for in this rapidly changing world.

—Don J. Usner, photo editor

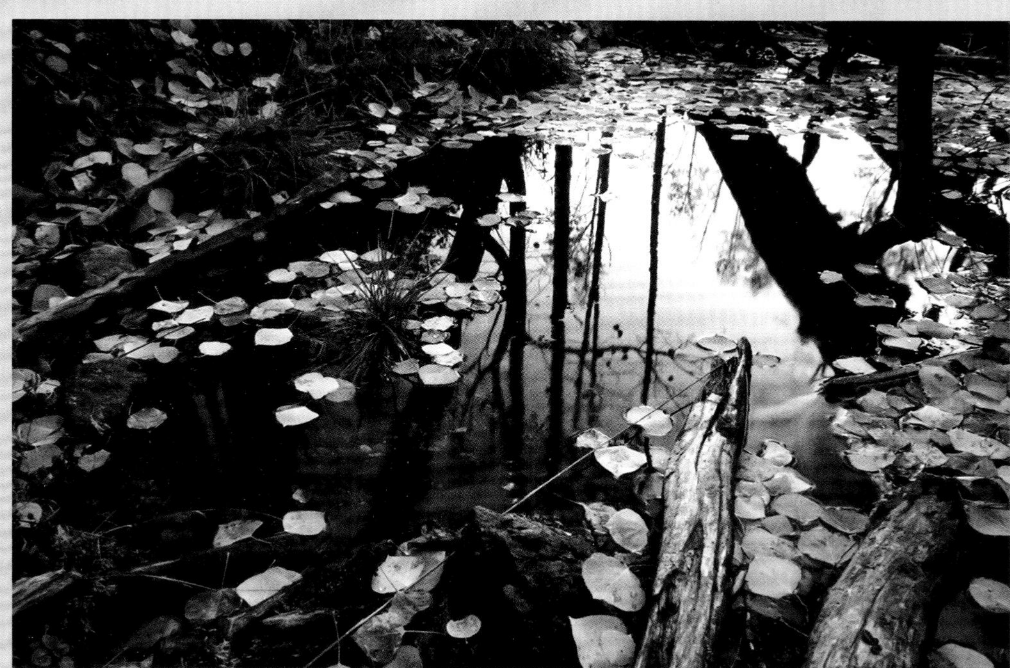

Aspen leaves and still water on a tributary of Tesuque Creek. Photograph by Don J. Usner.

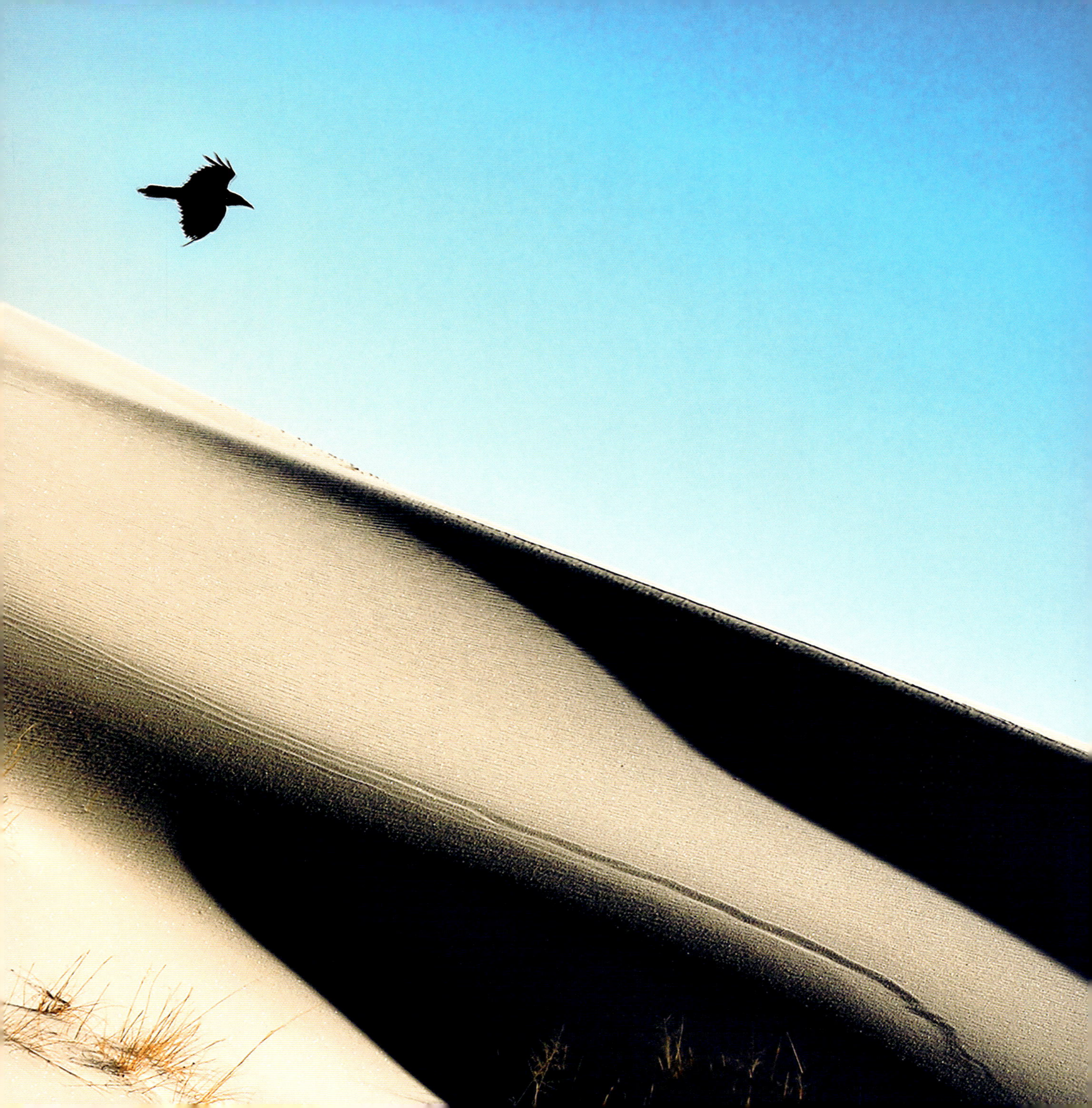

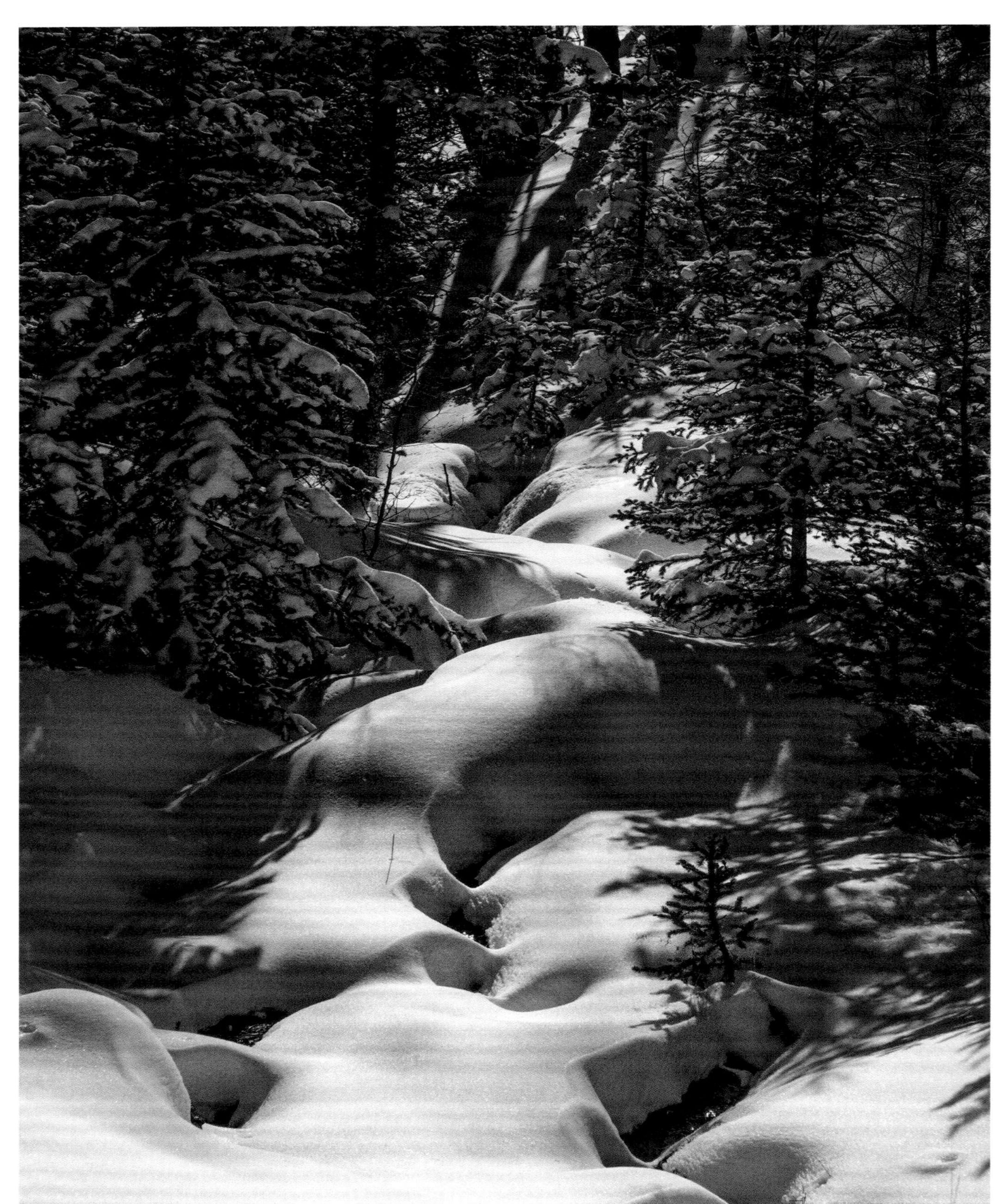

After a nighttime snowfall in
the Santa Fe National Forest.

David Halpern

January						
S	M	T	W	T	F	S
	1	2	3	4	5	6
7	8	9	10	11	12	13
14	15	16	17	18	19	20
21	22	23	24	25	26	27
28	29	30	31			

February						
S	M	T	W	T	F	S
				1	2	3
4	5	6	7	8	9	10
11	12	13	14	15	16	17
18	19	20	21	22	23	24
25	26	27	28	29		

January

1
Monday

New Year's Day

2
Tuesday

3
Wednesday

4
Thursday

5
Friday

6
Saturday

Epiphany
New Mexico Statehood Day (1912)

7
Sunday

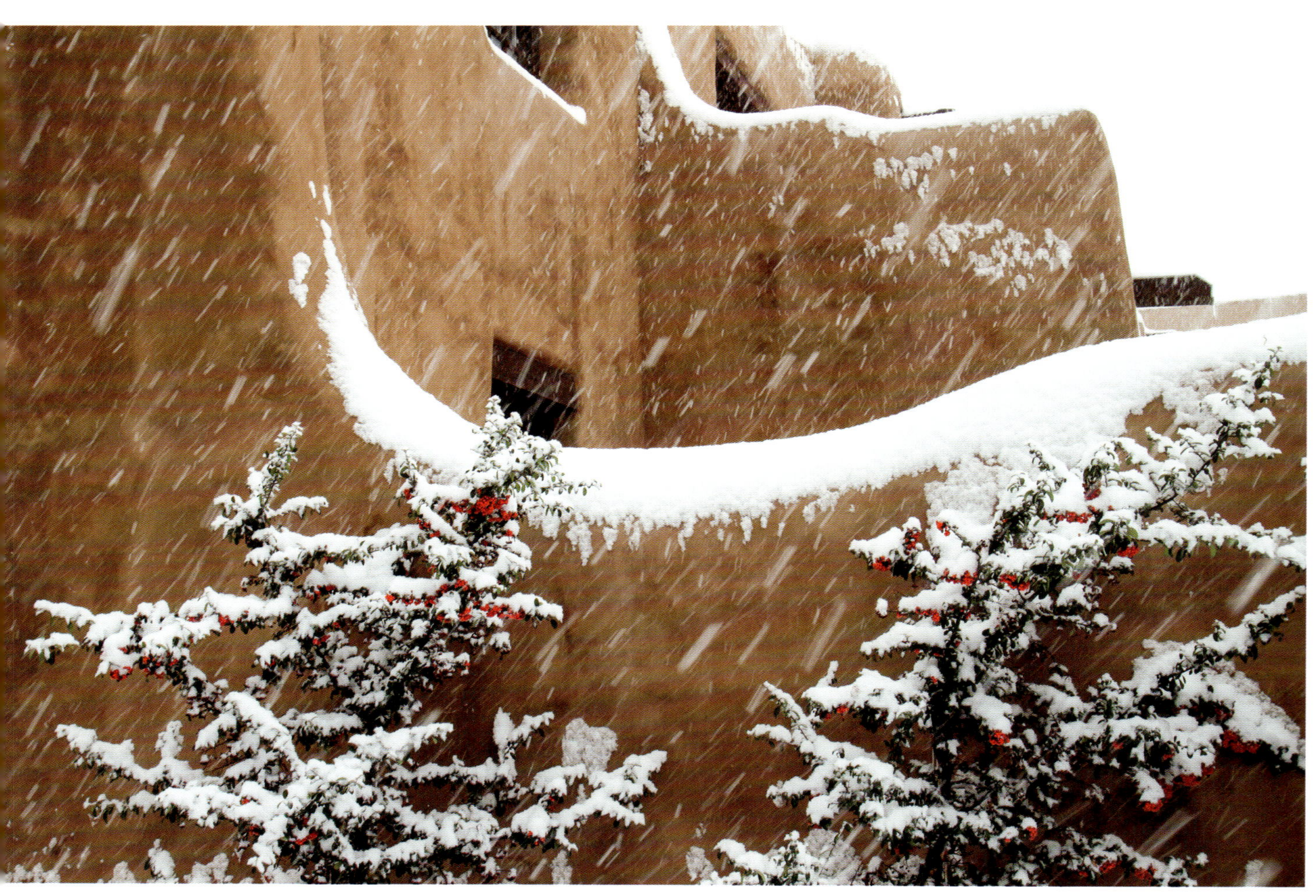

Snow blankets pyracantha and adobe walls of
the New Mexico Museum of Art in Santa Fe.

Bill Todino

January

8
Monday

9
Tuesday

10
Wednesday

● **11**
Thursday

12
Friday

13
Saturday

14
Sunday

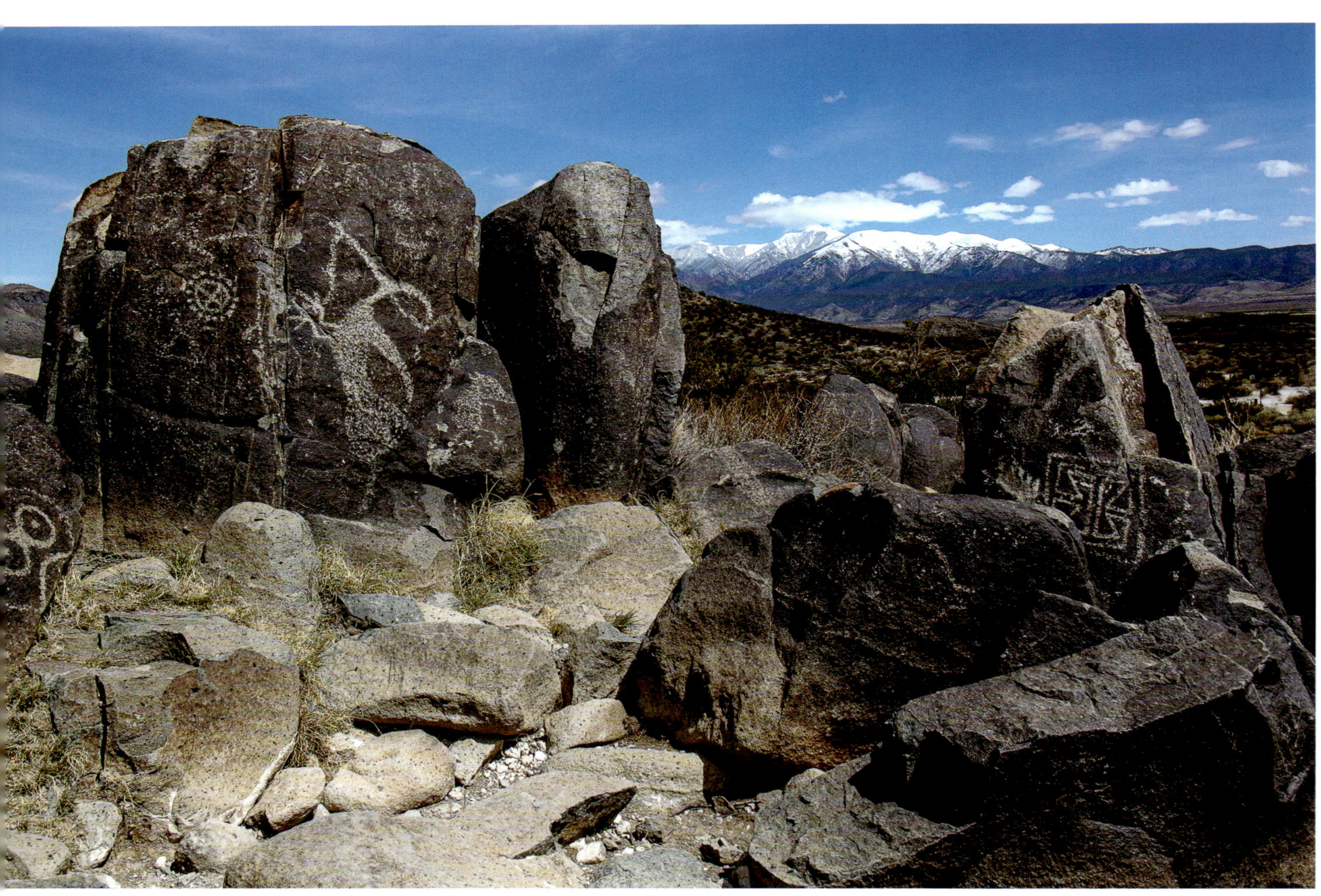

Three Rivers Petroglyph Site,
near Tularosa.

William Frej

January

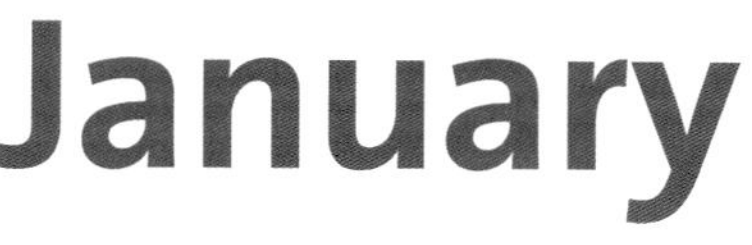

Martin Luther King Jr. Day

15
Monday

16
Tuesday

17
Wednesday

18
Thursday

19
Friday

20
Saturday

21
Sunday

January

S	M	T	W	T	F	S
	1	2	3	4	5	6
7	8	9	10	11	12	13
14	15	16	17	18	19	20
21	22	23	24	25	26	27
28	29	30	31			

February

S	M	T	W	T	F	S
				1	2	3
4	5	6	7	8	9	10
11	12	13	14	15	16	17
18	19	20	21	22	23	24
25	26	27	28	29		

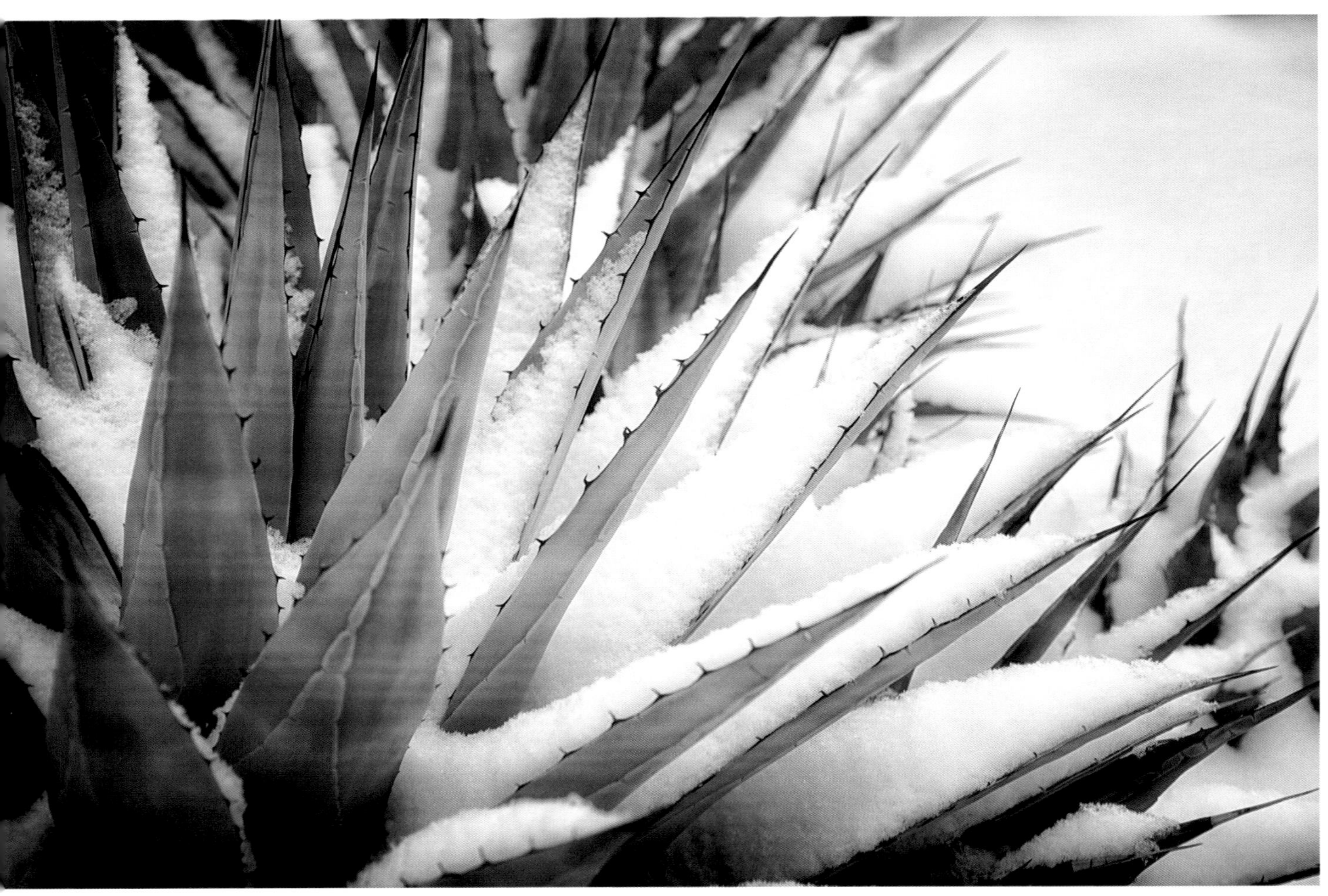

Taken in the photographer's garden in Albuquerque, the juxtaposition of soft snow on spiky agave.

Emma Eckert

22 Monday

23 Tuesday

24 Wednesday

25 Thursday

26 Friday

27 Saturday

28 Sunday

January 23   Tuesday

Pueblo de San Ildefonso Feast Day with Buffalo, Comanche, and Deer Dances, sanipueblo.org

January 25   Thursday

Taos Winter Wine Festival, at Taos Valley Ski Resort and other Taos venues, taoswinterwinefest.com (through January 28)

January

S	M	T	W	T	F	S
	1	2	3	4	5	6
7	8	9	10	11	12	13
14	15	16	17	18	19	20
21	22	23	24	25	26	27
28	29	30	31			

February

S	M	T	W	T	F	S
				1	2	3
4	5	6	7	8	9	10
11	12	13	14	15	16	17
18	19	20	21	22	23	24
25	26	27	28	29		

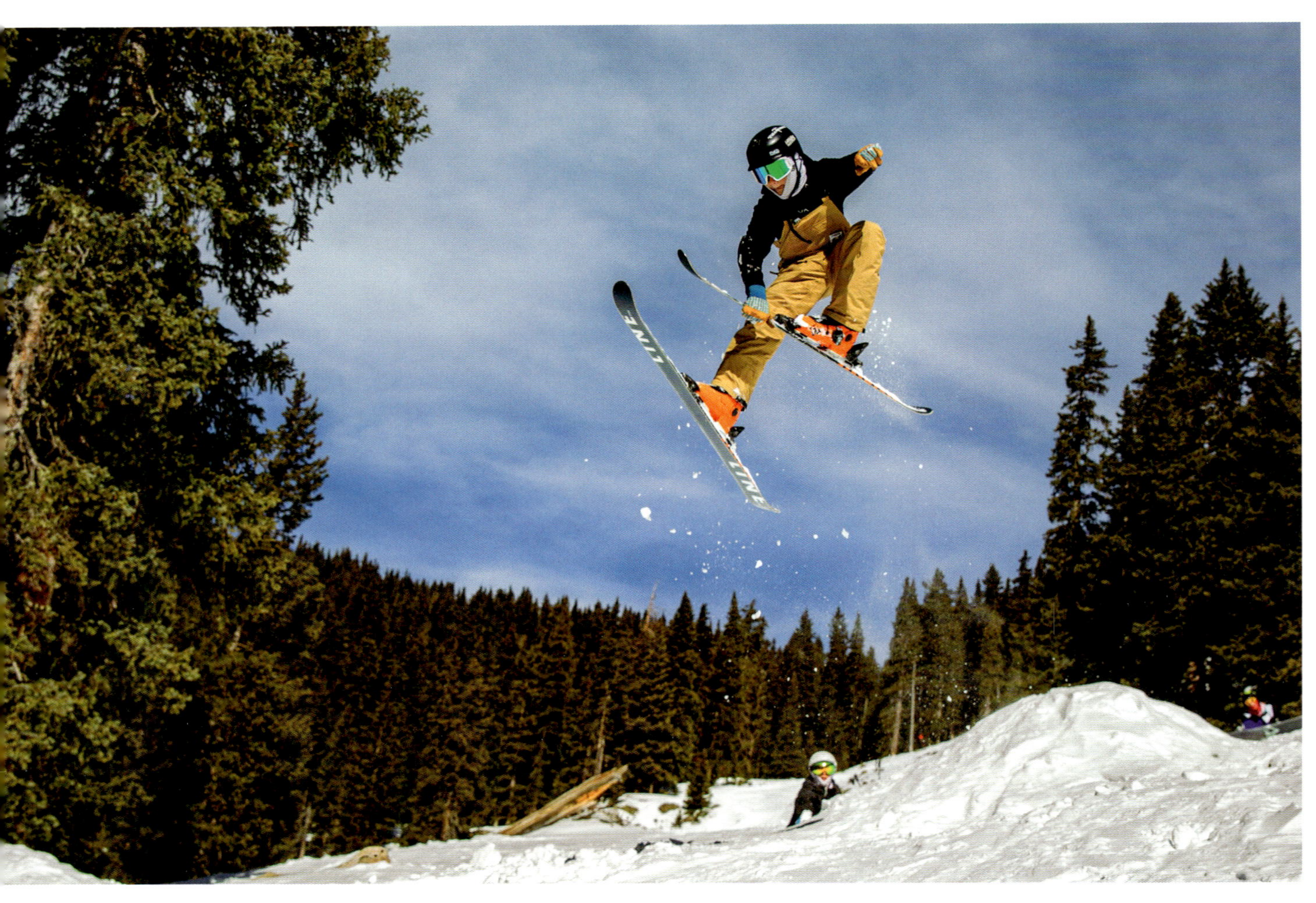

Ski jumping at Ski Santa Fe.

Zubin Stilling

January

29
Monday

30
Tuesday

31
Wednesday

February

1
Thursday

Black History Month

2
Friday

Groundhog Day
National Wear Red Day
◑

3
Saturday

4
Sunday

January

S	M	T	W	T	F	S
	1	2	3	4	5	6
7	8	9	10	11	12	13
14	15	16	17	18	19	20
21	22	23	24	25	26	27
28	29	30	31			

February

S	M	T	W	T	F	S
				1	2	3
4	5	6	7	8	9	10
11	12	13	14	15	16	17
18	19	20	21	22	23	24
25	26	27	28	29		

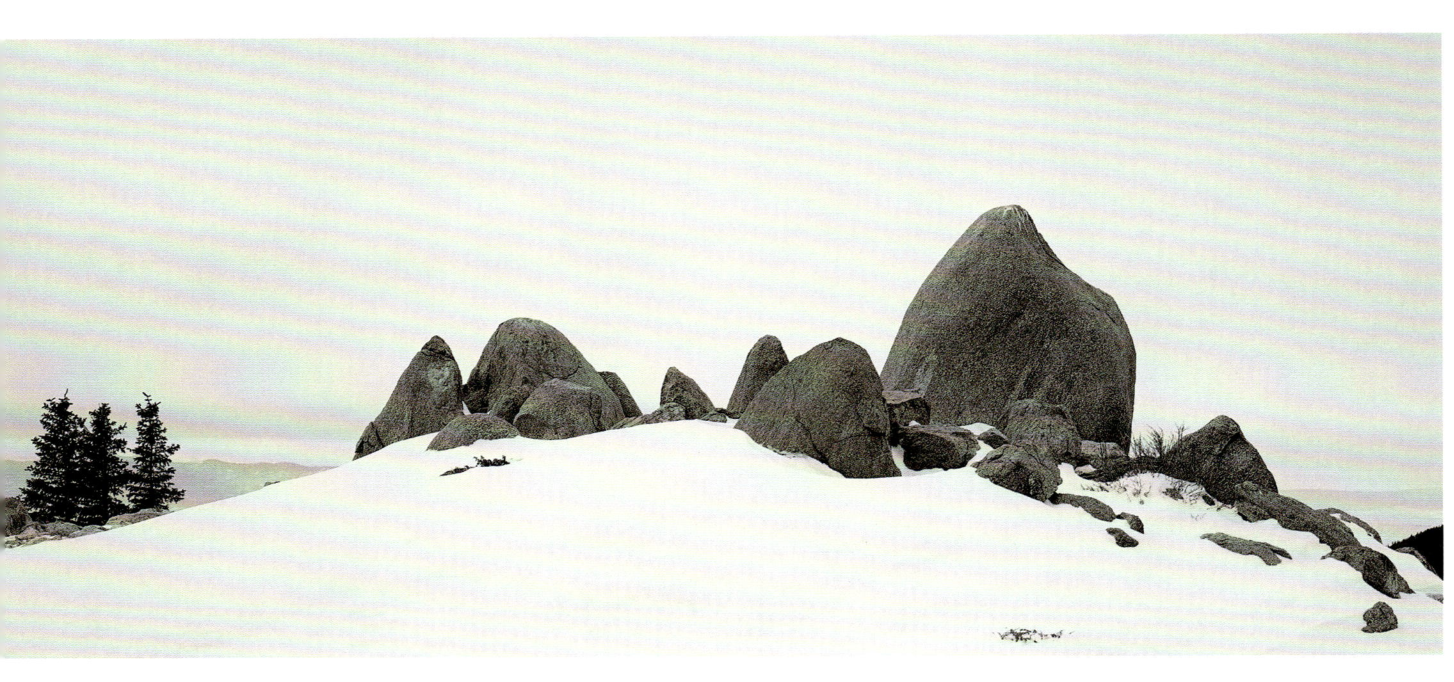

Winter, Sangre de Cristo
Mountains.

Scott Swearingen

February

5
Monday

6
Tuesday

7
Wednesday

8
Thursday

9
Friday

●

10
Saturday

Chinese New Year—Year of the Dragon

11
Sunday

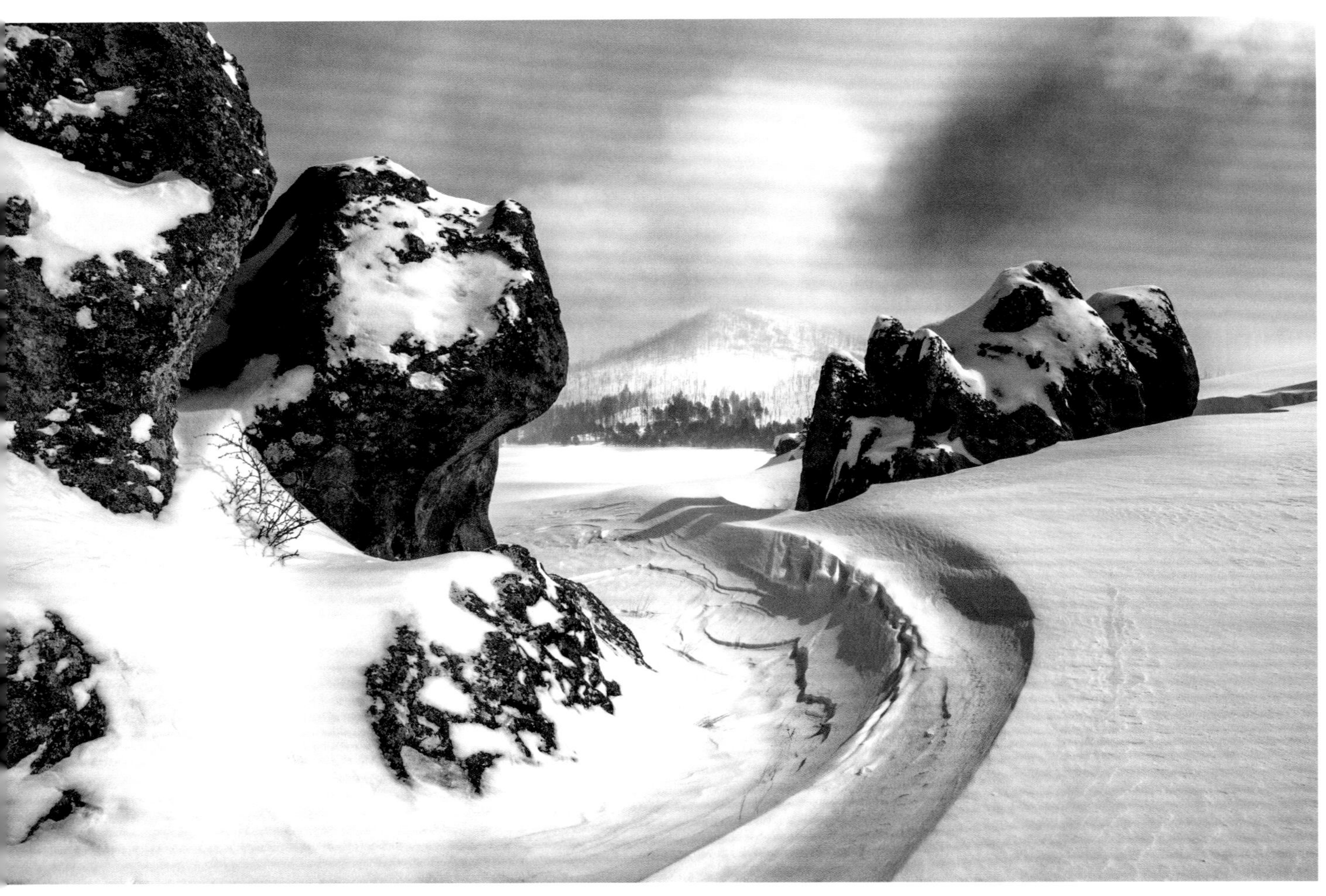

Snowdrifts, rocks, and Rabbit Mountain
in the Valle Grande, Valles Caldera
National Preserve.

Don J. Usner

Santa Fe Film Festival,
santafefilmfestival.com
(through February 25)

February

12
Monday

13
Tuesday

Mardi Gras

14
Wednesday

Valentine's Day
Ash Wednesday

15
Thursday

16
Friday

◑

17
Saturday

18
Sunday

February						
S	M	T	W	T	F	S
				1	2	3
4	5	6	7	8	9	10
11	12	13	14	15	16	17
18	19	20	21	22	23	24
25	26	27	28	29		

March						
S	M	T	W	T	F	S
					1	2
3	4	5	6	7	8	9
10	11	12	13	14	15	16
17	18	19	20	21	22	23
24	25	26	27	28	29	30
31						

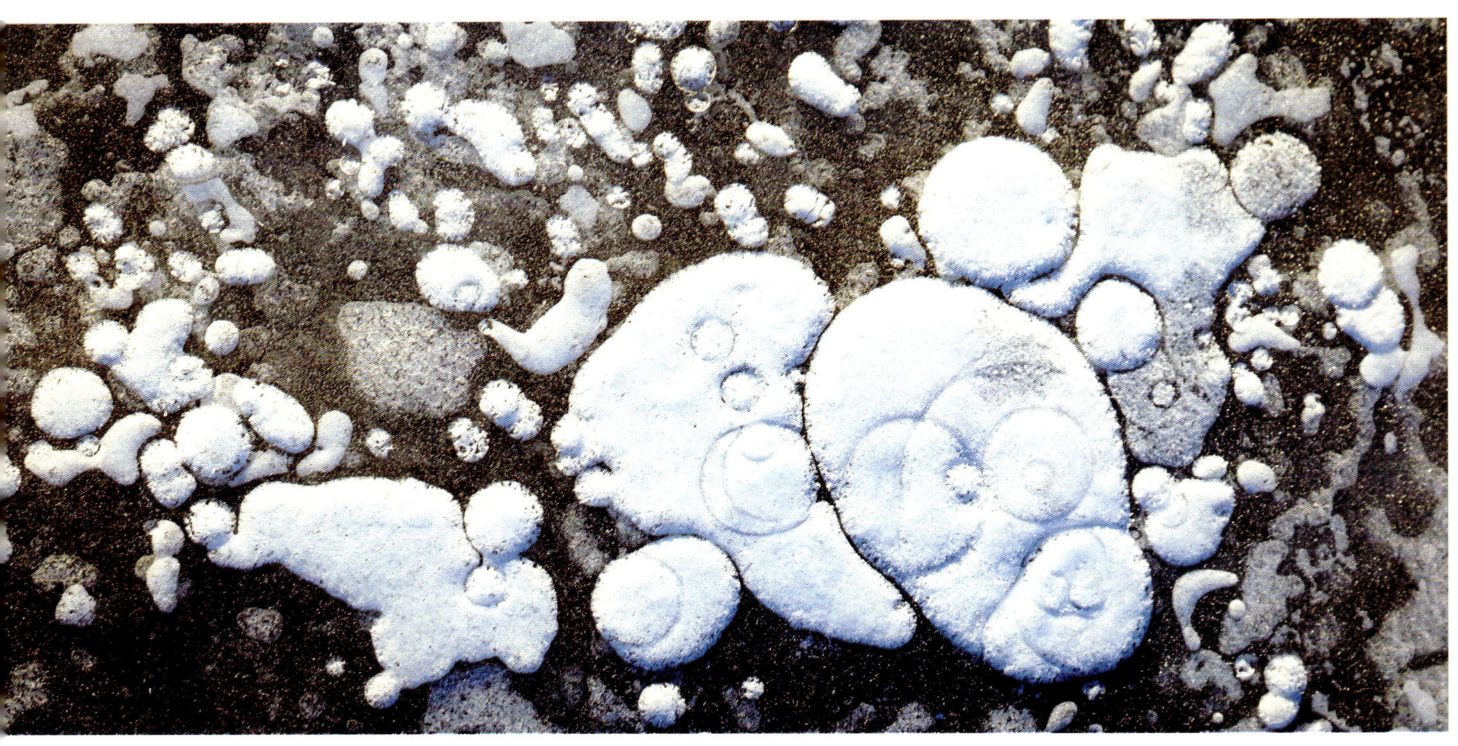

Ice, snow, and wind etch shapes and faces into
the frozen surface of the Rio Chama, near the
Monastery of Christ in the Desert, Abiquiu.

Brian VanDenzen

February

19
Monday

Presidents Day (Washington's Birthday)

20
Tuesday

21
Wednesday

22
Thursday

National Margarita Day

23
Friday

24
Saturday

○

25
Sunday

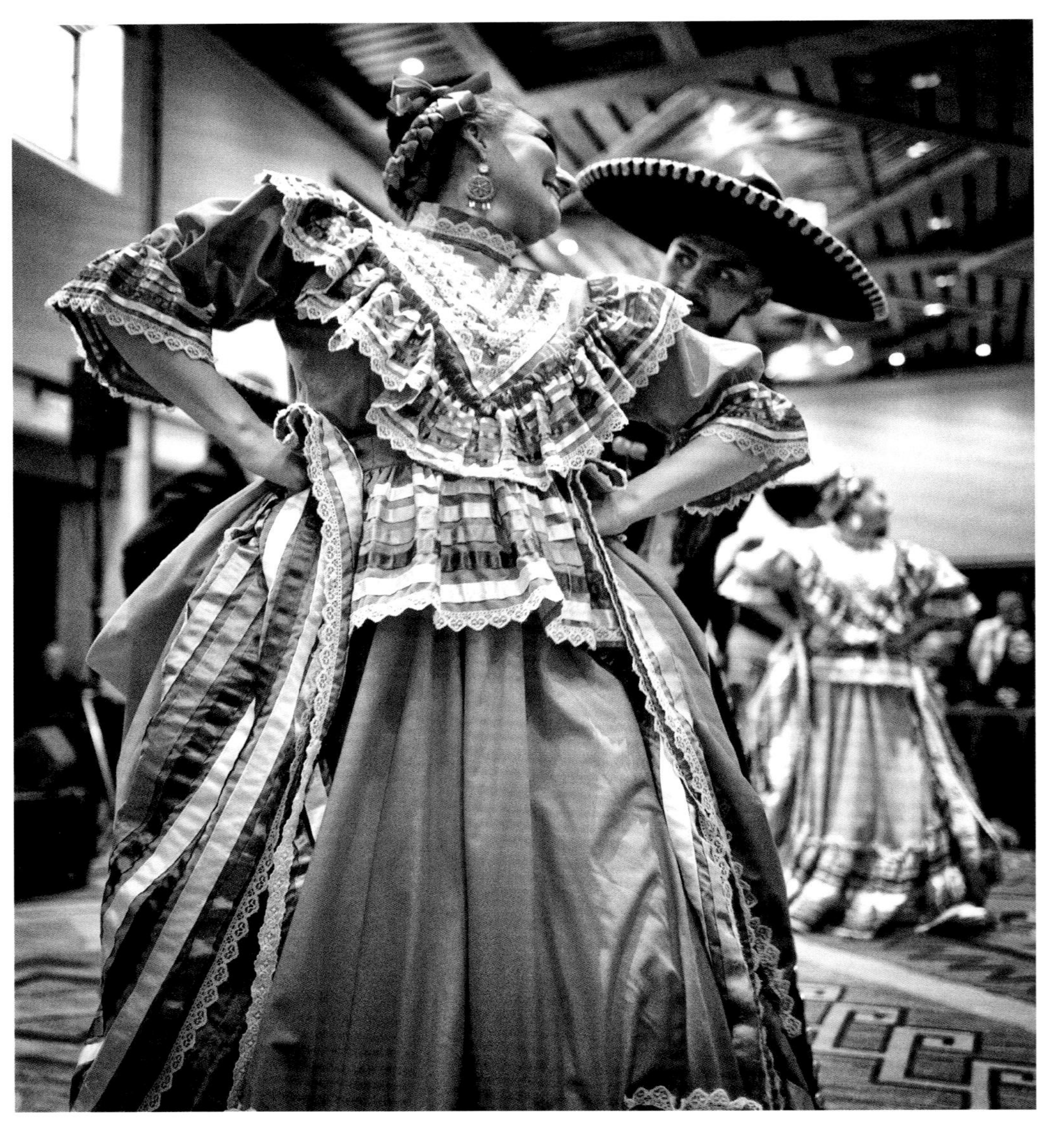

Folkloric dancers from Los Niños de Santa Fe perform at the Traditional Spanish Market Artists Show in Santa Fe.

Don J. Usner

National Fiery Foods & Barbecue Show in Albuquerque, fieryfoodsshow.com (through March 3)

February

26
Monday

27
Tuesday

28
Wednesday

29
Thursday

March

Women's History Month
Employee Appreciation Day

1
Friday

Read Across America Day

2
Saturday

◑

3
Sunday

February

S	M	T	W	T	F	S
				1	2	3
4	5	6	7	8	9	10
11	12	13	14	15	16	17
18	19	20	21	22	23	24
25	26	27	28	29		

March

S	M	T	W	T	F	S
					1	2
3	4	5	6	7	8	9
10	11	12	13	14	15	16
17	18	19	20	21	22	23
24	25	26	27	28	29	30
31						

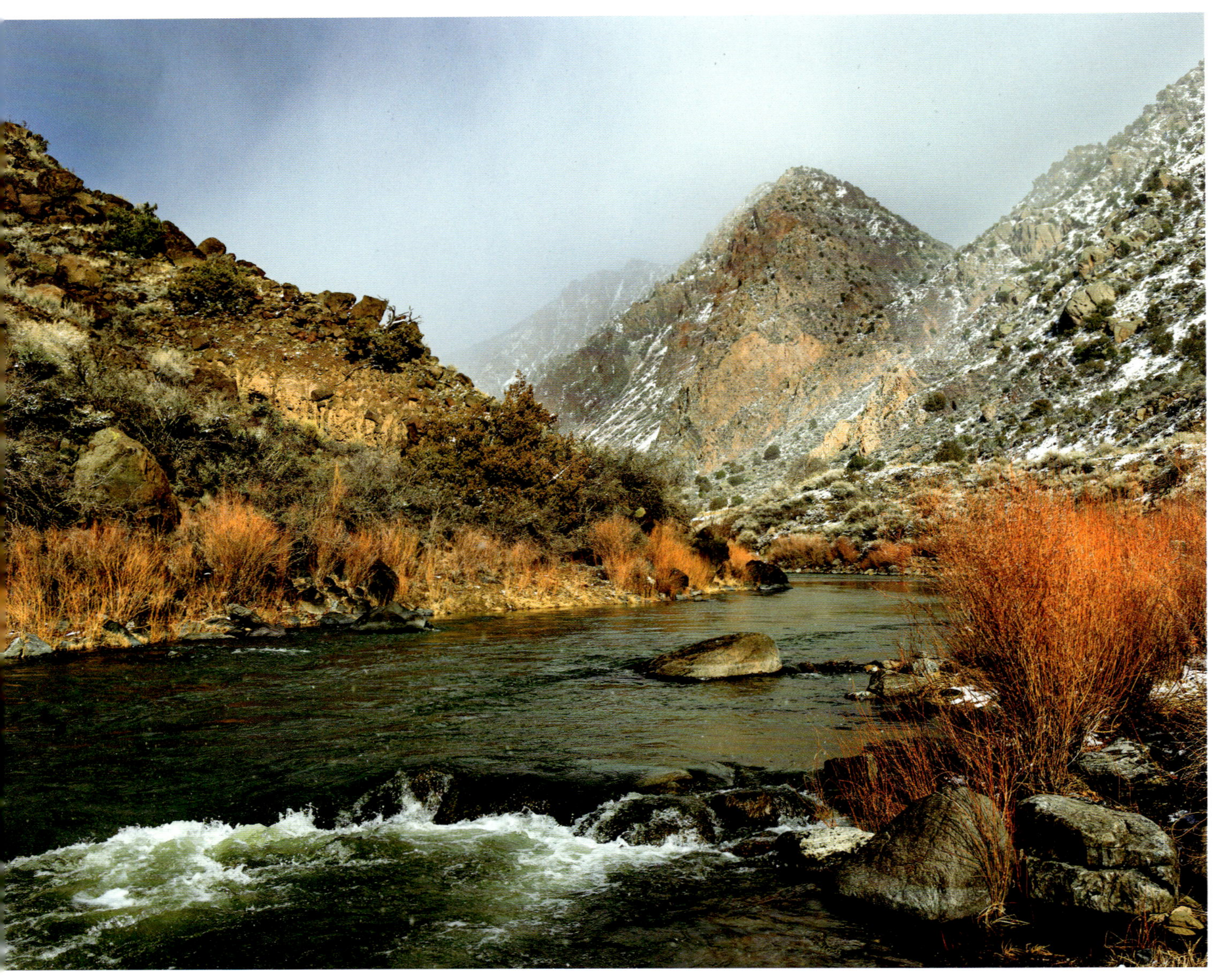

Snowflakes fill the sky and descend to the river bottom of the Rio Grande Gorge near Pilar.

Brian VanDenzen

March

4 Monday

5 Tuesday

6 Wednesday

7 Thursday

International Women's Day

8 Friday

9 Saturday

Daylight Saving Time begins
Ramadan (begins sundown March 10 and ends nightfall April 8)
●

10 Sunday

March

S	M	T	W	T	F	S
					1	2
3	4	5	6	7	8	9
10	11	12	13	14	15	16
17	18	19	20	21	22	23
24	25	26	27	28	29	30
31						

April

S	M	T	W	T	F	S
	1	2	3	4	5	6
7	8	9	10	11	12	13
14	15	16	17	18	19	20
21	22	23	24	25	26	27
28	29	30				

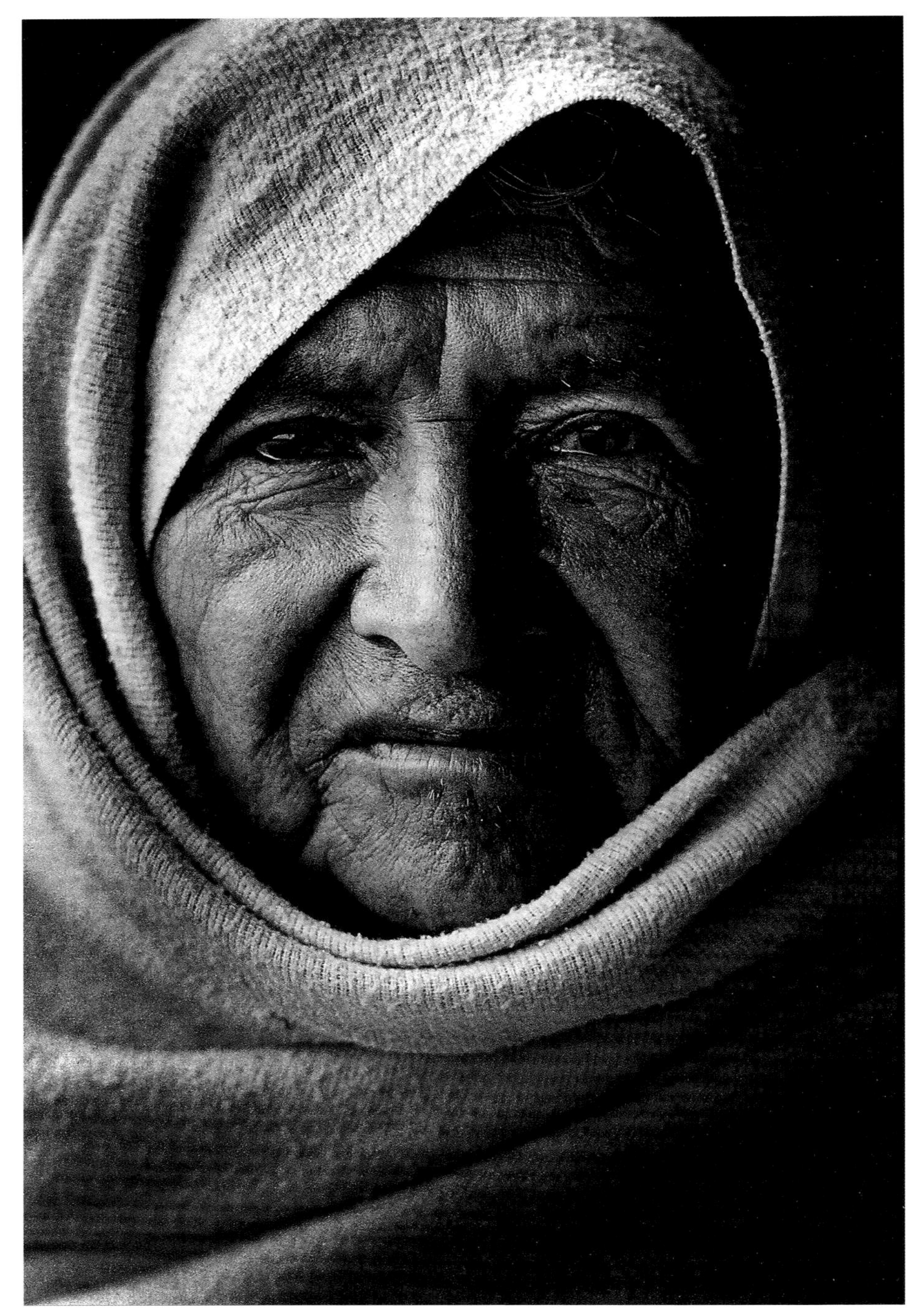

Taos Elder.

Jim Arndt

Bataan Memorial Death March,
White Sands Missile Range,
bataanmarch.com

March

11
Monday

12
Tuesday

13
Wednesday

14
Thursday

15
Friday

16
Saturday

17
Sunday

St. Patrick's Day

March

S	M	T	W	T	F	S
					1	2
3	4	5	6	7	8	9
10	11	12	13	14	15	16
17	18	19	20	21	22	23
24	25	26	27	28	29	30
31						

April

S	M	T	W	T	F	S
	1	2	3	4	5	6
7	8	9	10	11	12	13
14	15	16	17	18	19	20
21	22	23	24	25	26	27
28	29	30				

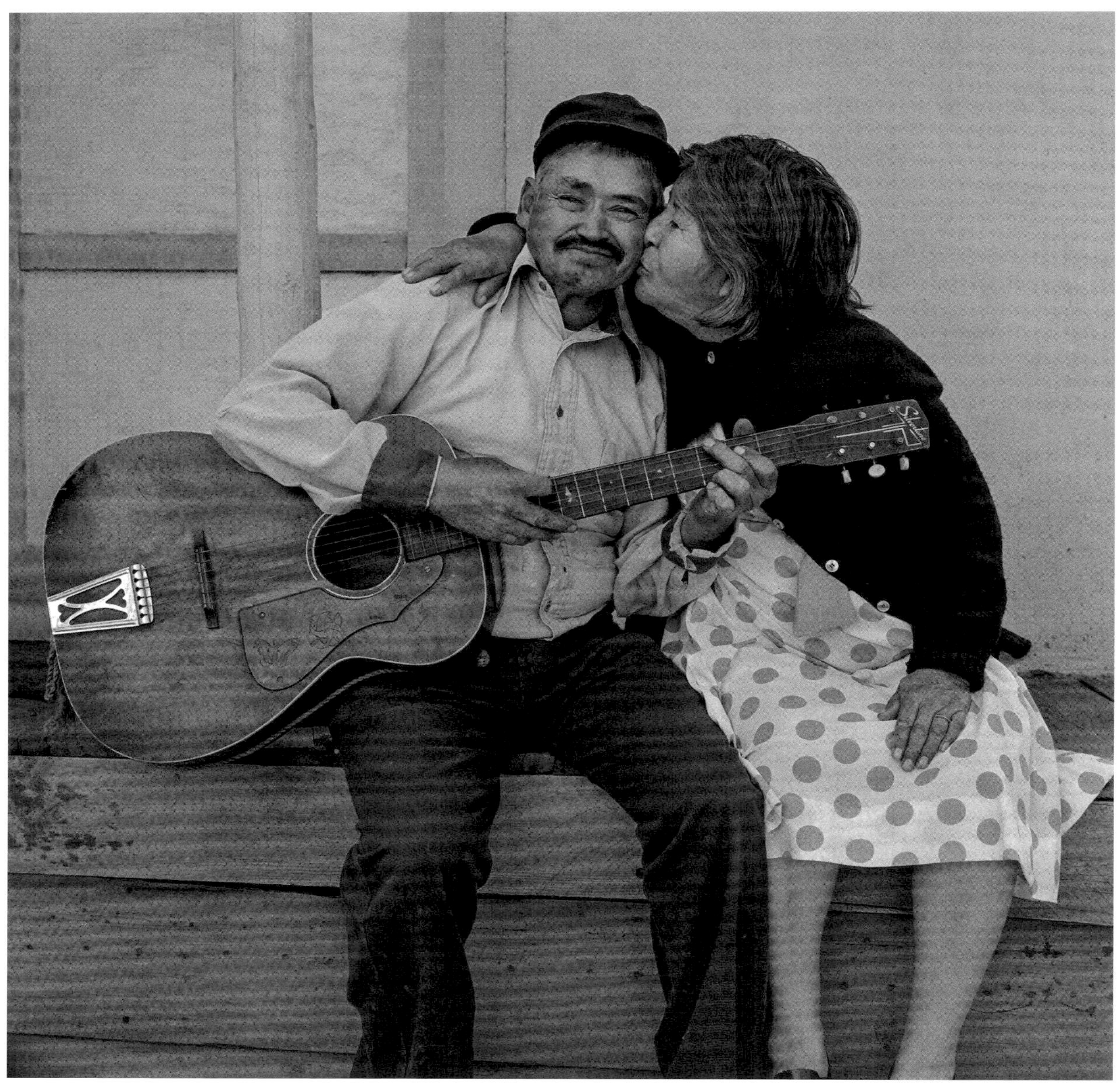

Onesimo and Eleanor Pacheco
at home in Vallecito.

Alex Harris

March 19   Tuesday

St. Joseph's Feast Day with Harvest and various dances at Laguna Pueblo (Old Laguna), lagunapueblo-nsn.gov

March

S	M	T	W	T	F	S
					1	2
3	4	5	6	7	8	9
10	11	12	13	14	15	16
17	18	19	20	21	22	23
24	25	26	27	28	29	30
31						

April

S	M	T	W	T	F	S
	1	2	3	4	5	6
7	8	9	10	11	12	13
14	15	16	17	18	19	20
21	22	23	24	25	26	27
28	29	30				

18
Monday

19
Tuesday

Spring Equinox

20
Wednesday

International Day of Happiness

21
Thursday

22
Friday

23
Saturday

24
Sunday

Palm Sunday

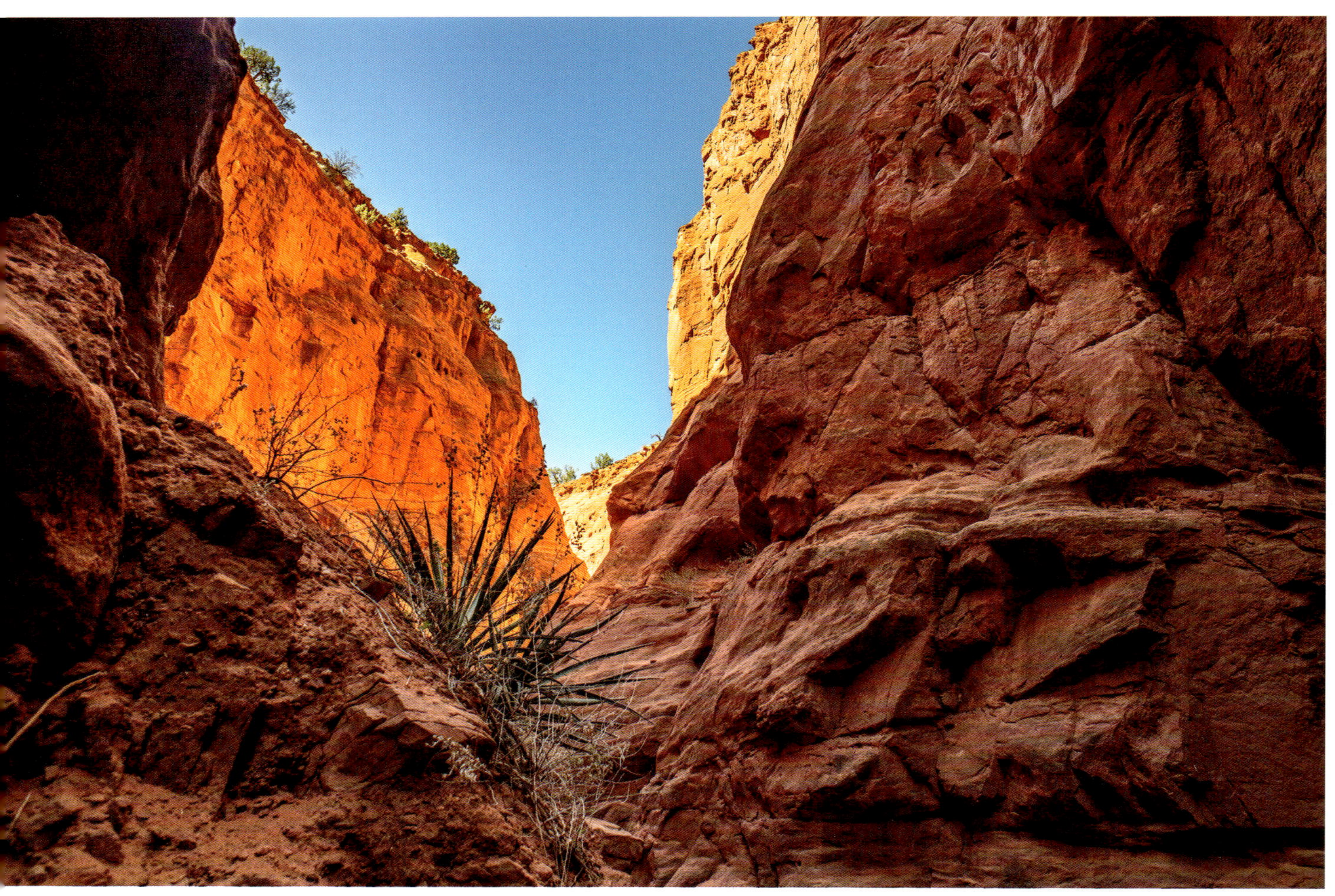

These red sandstone rocks deposited by an ancient river have become an iconic image connected with Jemez Pueblo.

Theodore Greer

Various dances at most pueblos,
indianpueblo.org/feast-days/

March

25
Monday

Holi
○

26
Tuesday

27
Wednesday

28
Thursday

Good Friday
National Vietnam War Veterans Day

29
Friday

Holy Saturday

30
Saturday

Easter
César Chávez Day
International Day of Transgender Visibility

31
Sunday

March

S	M	T	W	T	F	S
					1	2
3	4	5	6	7	8	9
10	11	12	13	14	15	16
17	18	19	20	21	22	23
24	25	26	27	28	29	30
31						

April

S	M	T	W	T	F	S
	1	2	3	4	5	6
7	8	9	10	11	12	13
14	15	16	17	18	19	20
21	22	23	24	25	26	27
28	29	30				

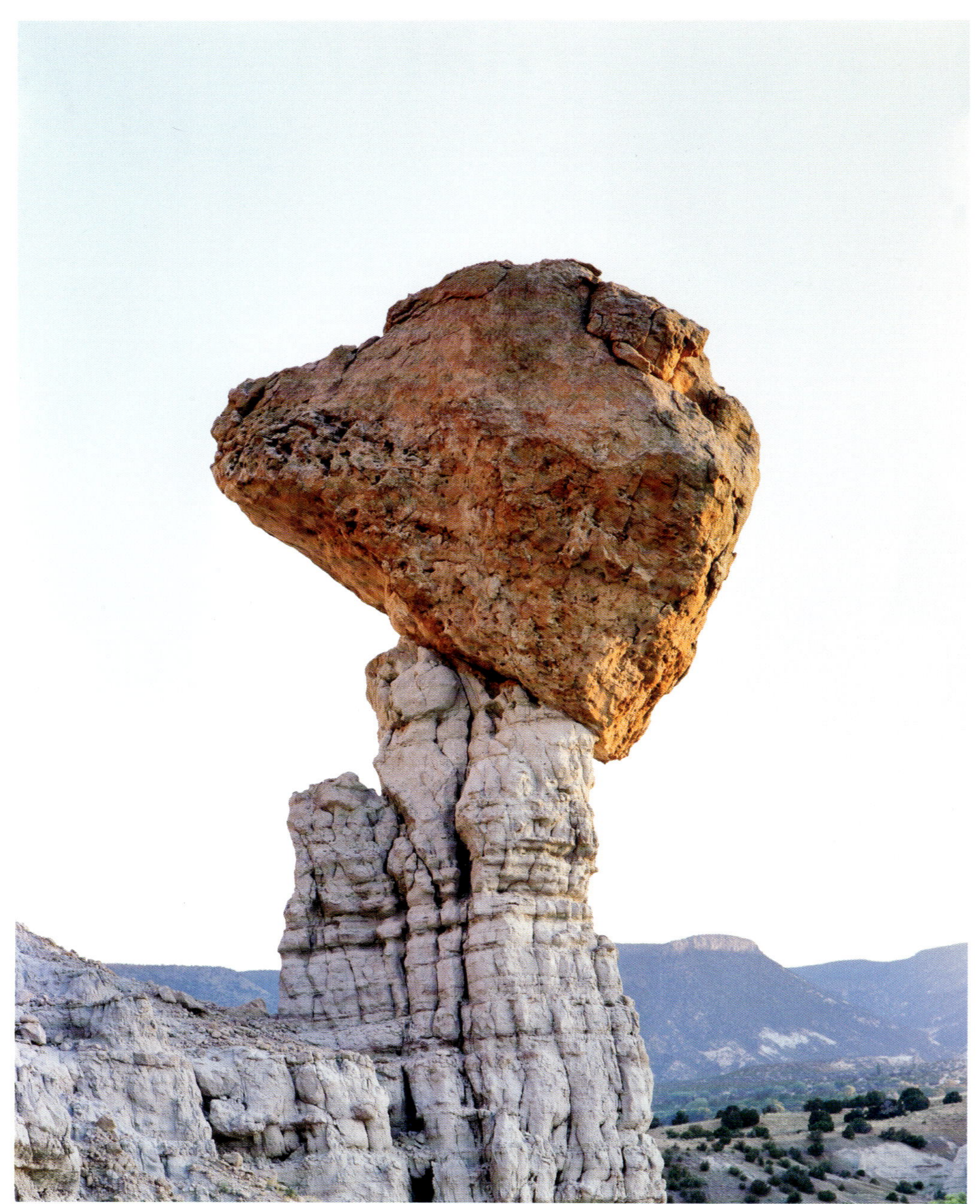

Rock-solid in Abiquiu.

Peter Ogilvie

National Library Week begins
(through April 13, ala.org)

April

April Fool's Day
National Poetry Month
◑

1
Monday

2
Tuesday

3
Wednesday

4
Thursday

5
Friday

6
Saturday

7
Sunday

April

S	M	T	W	T	F	S
	1	2	3	4	5	6
7	8	9	10	11	12	13
14	15	16	17	18	19	20
21	22	23	24	25	26	27
28	29	30				

May

S	M	T	W	T	F	S
			1	2	3	4
5	6	7	8	9	10	11
12	13	14	15	16	17	18
19	20	21	22	23	24	25
26	27	28	29	30	31	

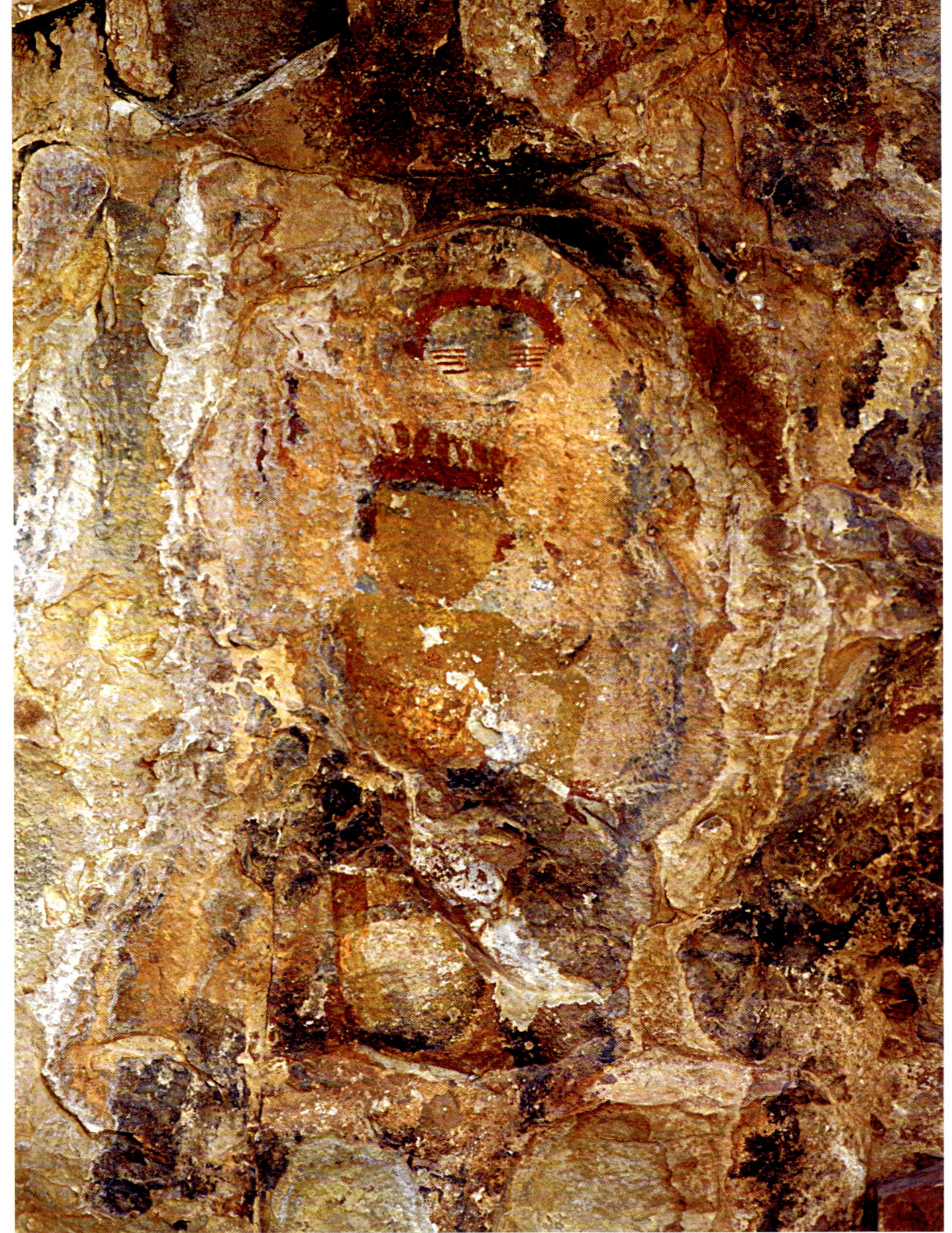

Tompiro Culture rock
paintings of Kachina
masks and dancer,
Manzano Mountains.

Bob Young

April

8
Monday

●

9
Tuesday

National Library Workers Day
Eid al-Fitr (begins sundown today and ends nightfall on April 10)

10
Wednesday

11
Thursday

12
Friday

13
Saturday

14
Sunday

April

S	M	T	W	T	F	S
	1	2	3	4	5	6
7	8	9	10	11	12	13
14	15	16	17	18	19	20
21	22	23	24	25	26	27
28	29	30				

May

S	M	T	W	T	F	S
			1	2	3	4
5	6	7	8	9	10	11
12	13	14	15	16	17	18
19	20	21	22	23	24	25
26	27	28	29	30	31	

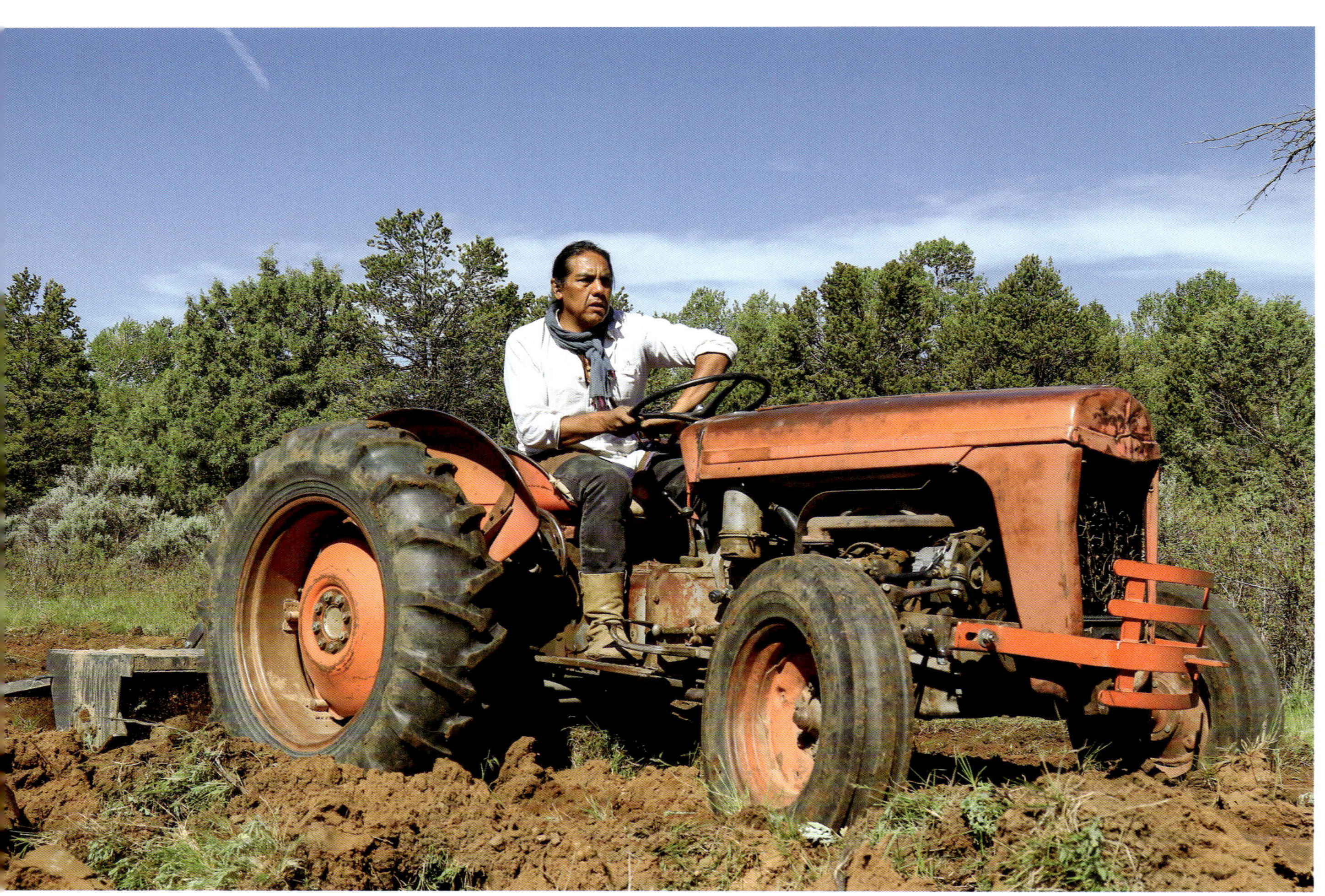

Robert Mirabal of Tewa Farms in Taos,
getting the earth ready for the Blue Corn maidens.

Bill Curry

April

15
Monday

◐

16
Tuesday

Tax Day

17
Wednesday

18
Thursday

19
Friday

20
Saturday

21
Sunday

April

S	M	T	W	T	F	S
	1	2	3	4	5	6
7	8	9	10	11	12	13
14	15	16	17	18	19	20
21	22	23	24	25	26	27
28	29	30				

May

S	M	T	W	T	F	S
			1	2	3	4
5	6	7	8	9	10	11
12	13	14	15	16	17	18
19	20	21	22	23	24	25
26	27	28	29	30	31	

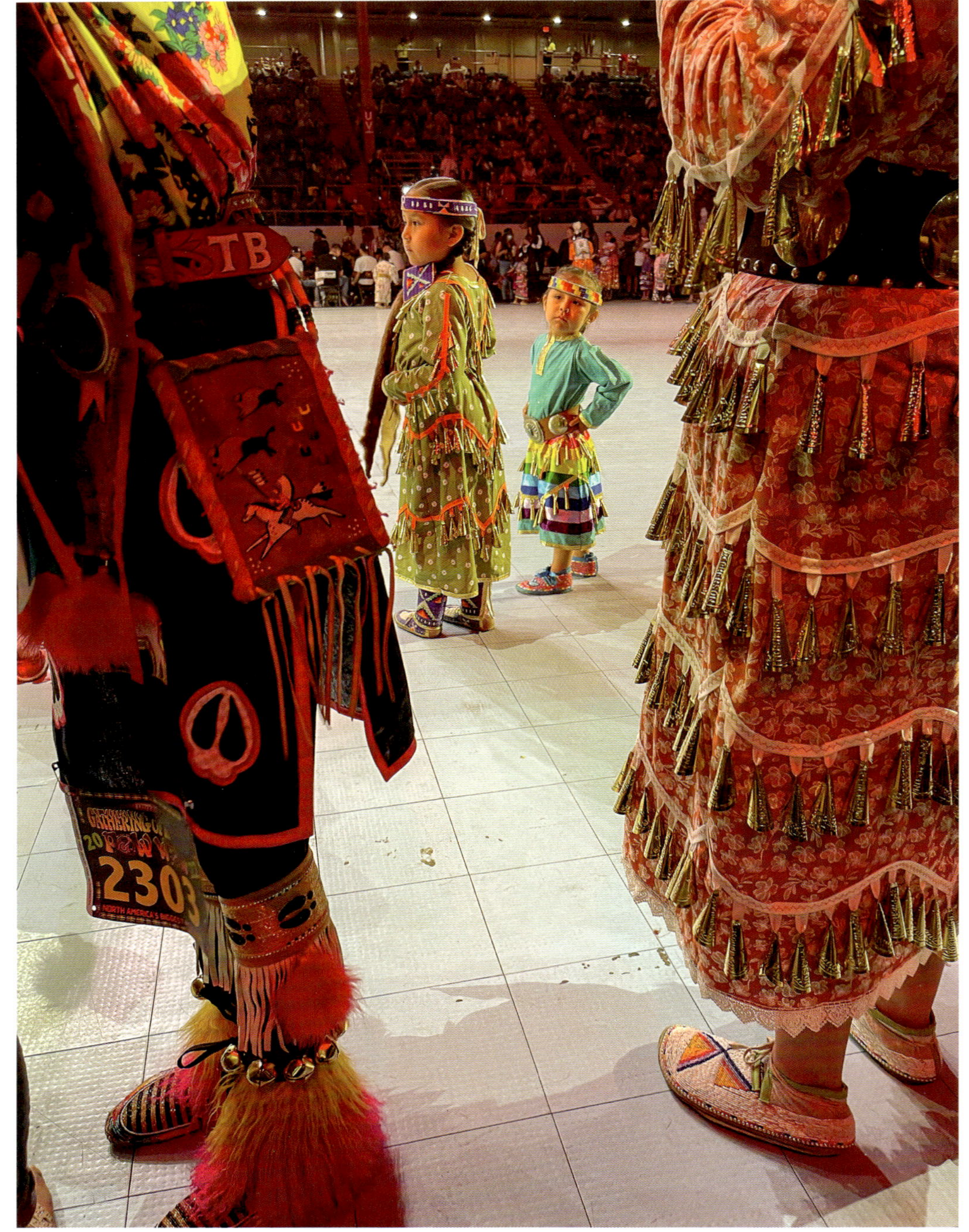

Gathering of Nations,
Albuquerque.

Evalyn Bemis

Gathering of Nations Powwow begins, gatheringofnations.com (through April 28)

April

22
Monday

Passover (begins sundown April 22 and ends nightfall April 30)

23
Tuesday

World Book Day

24
Wednesday

Earth Day
Administrative Professionals Day

25
Thursday

Take Our Children to Work Day

26
Friday

Arbor Day

27
Saturday

28
Sunday

April

S	M	T	W	T	F	S
	1	2	3	4	5	6
7	8	9	10	11	12	13
14	15	16	17	18	19	20
21	22	23	24	25	26	27
28	29	30				

May

S	M	T	W	T	F	S
			1	2	3	4
5	6	7	8	9	10	11
12	13	14	15	16	17	18
19	20	21	22	23	24	25
26	27	28	29	30	31	

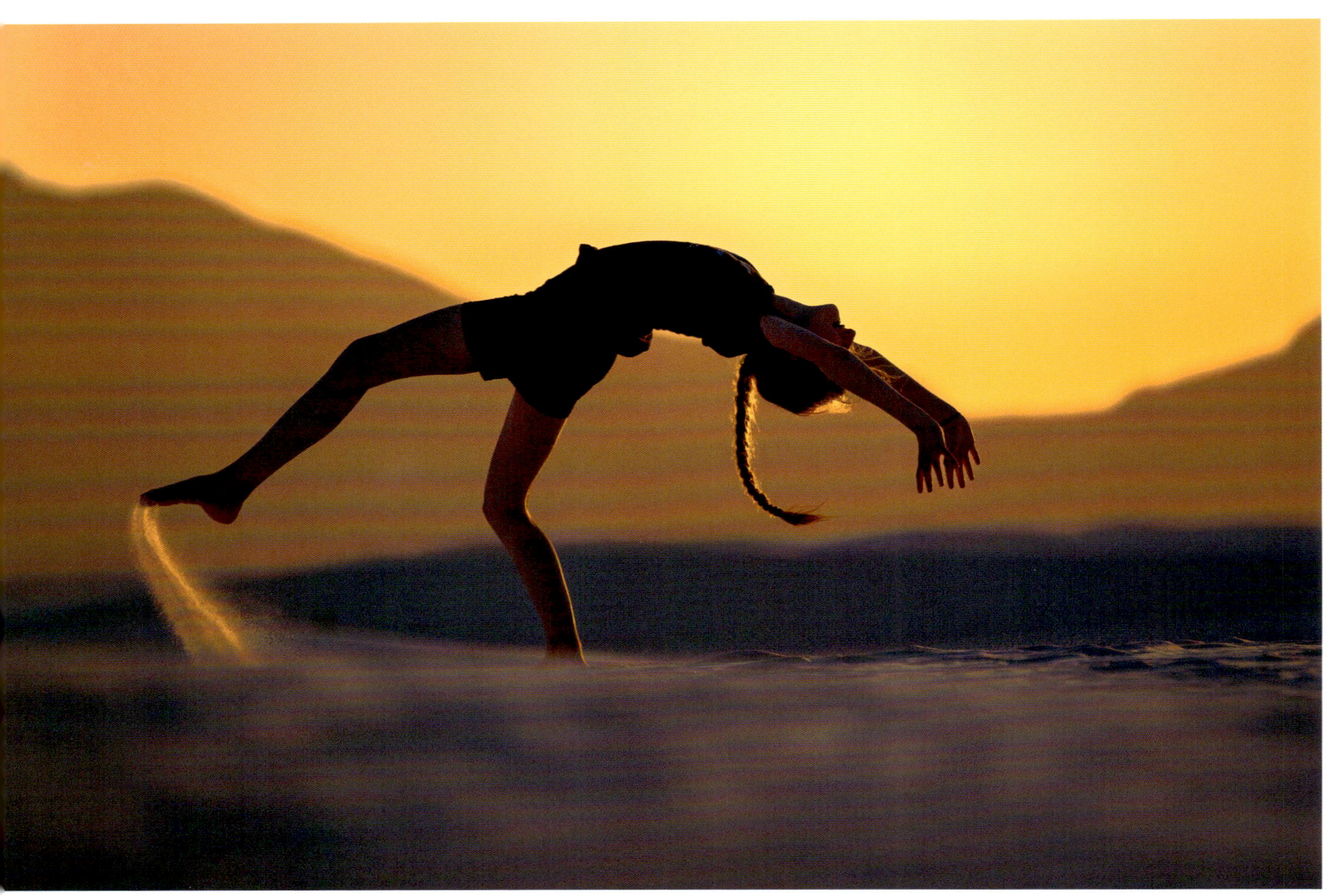

Gymnastics on the dunes of White Sands.

Zubin Stillings

April

29
Monday

30
Tuesday

May

1
May Day
Wednesday

2
Thursday

3
Friday

4
Saturday

5
Cinco de Mayo
Sunday

April						
S	M	T	W	T	F	S
	1	2	3	4	5	6
7	8	9	10	11	12	13
14	15	16	17	18	19	20
21	22	23	24	25	26	27
28	29	30				

May						
S	M	T	W	T	F	S
			1	2	3	4
5	6	7	8	9	10	11
12	13	14	15	16	17	18
19	20	21	22	23	24	25
26	27	28	29	30	31	

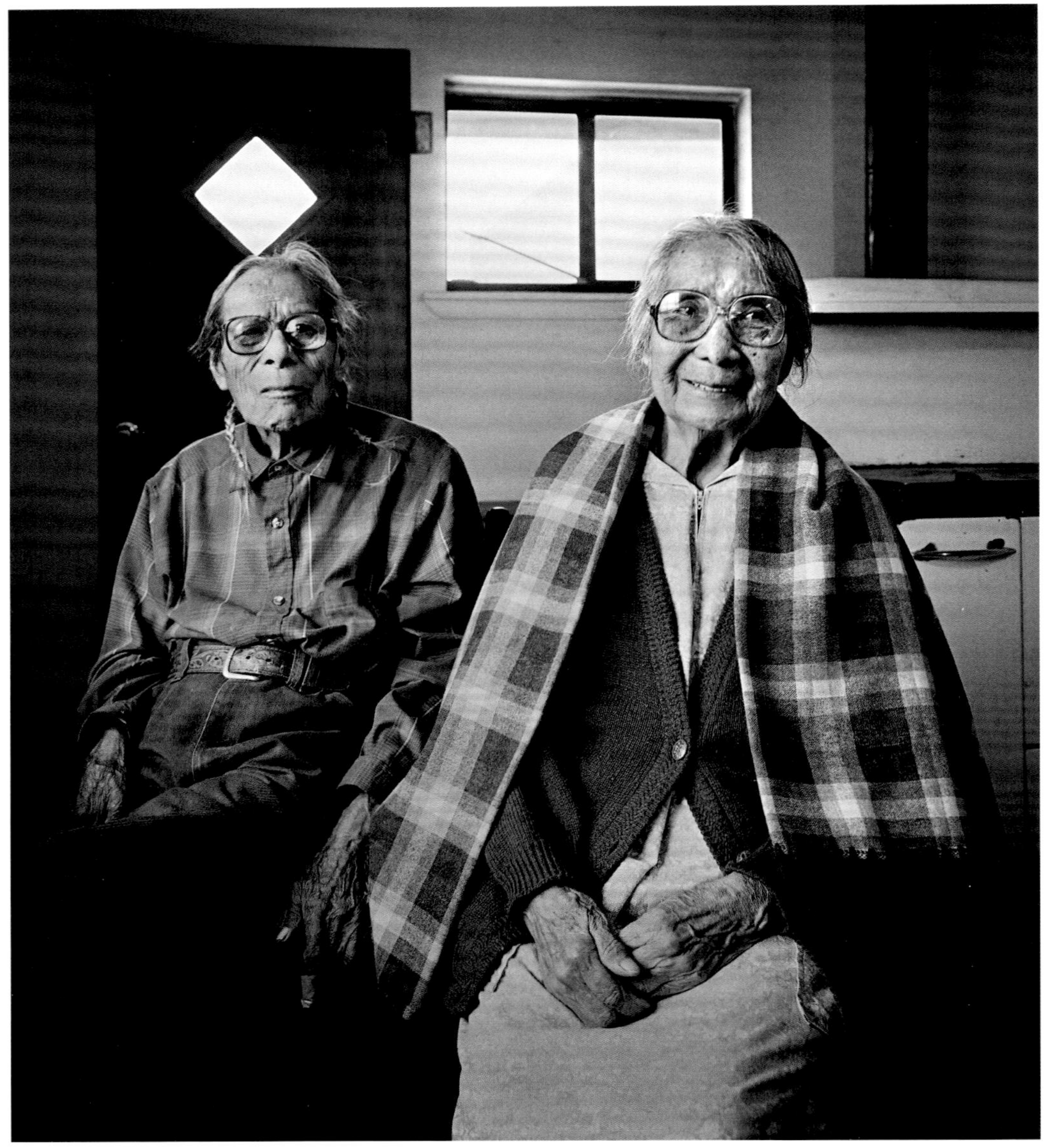

Adam and Santina Martinez, in the kitchen of their San Ildefonso home, 1995.
The two were named Santa Fe Living Treasures. Adam was the oldest son of
San Ildefonso pueblo potter Maria Martinez.

Steve Northup

Mother's Day Whitewater Races,
Rio Grande Racecourse in Pilar,
mothersdaywhitewater.com

May

6
Monday

National Nurses Day

7
Tuesday

●

8
Wednesday

9
Thursday

10
Friday

11
Saturday

12
Sunday

Mother's Day

May

S	M	T	W	T	F	S
			1	2	3	4
5	6	7	8	9	10	11
12	13	14	15	16	17	18
19	20	21	22	23	24	25
26	27	28	29	30	31	

June

S	M	T	W	T	F	S
						1
2	3	4	5	6	7	8
9	10	11	12	13	14	15
16	17	18	19	20	21	22
23	24	25	26	27	28	29
30						

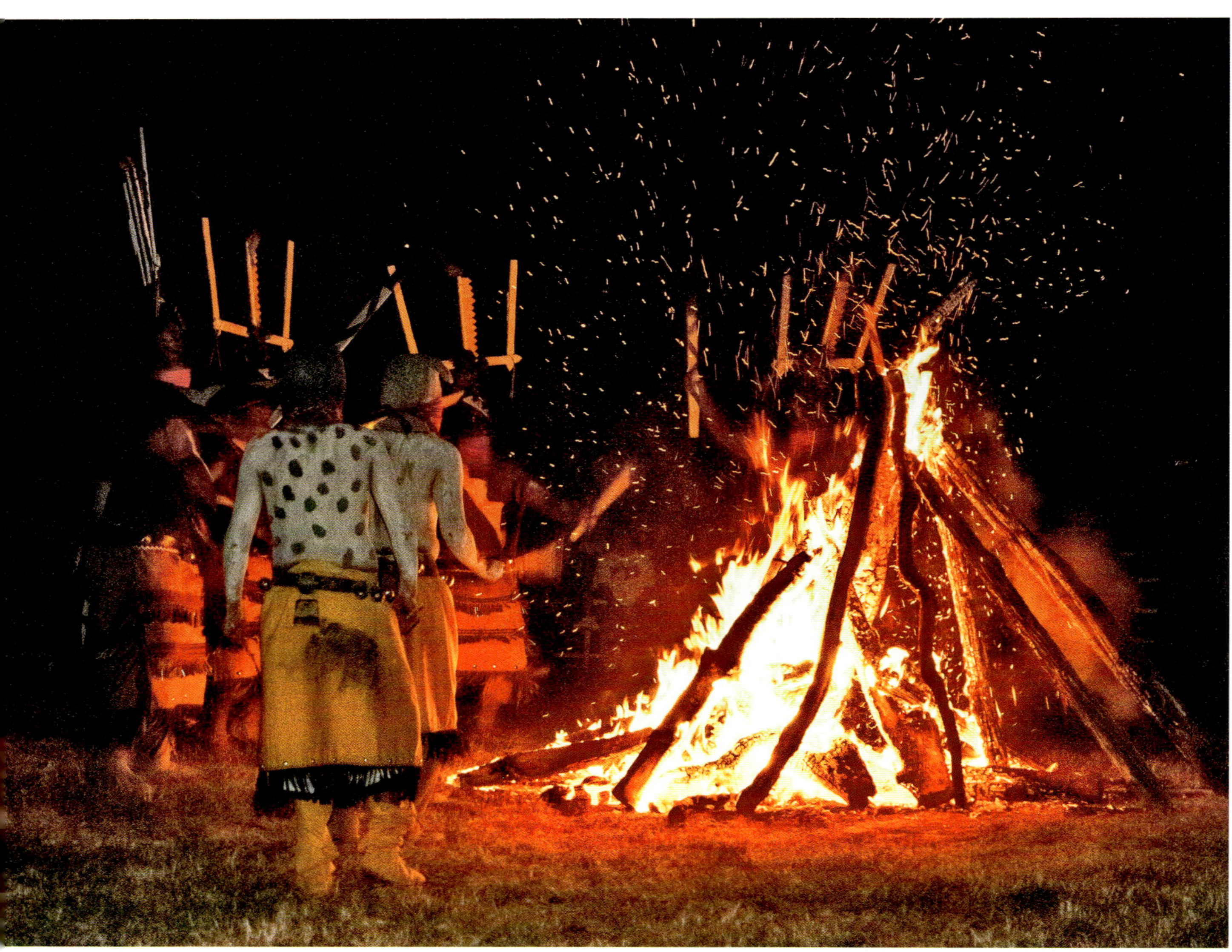

Apache Dance of the Mountain Gods at the
Living Desert Zoo & Gardens in Carlsbad.

Judy McGowan

May

Santa Fe International Literary Festival (through May 19), sfinternationallitfest.org

13
Monday

14
Tuesday

15
Wednesday

16
Thursday

17
Friday

18
Saturday

Armed Forces Day
International Museum Day

19
Sunday

May

S	M	T	W	T	F	S
			1	2	3	4
5	6	7	8	9	10	11
12	13	14	15	16	17	18
19	20	21	22	23	24	25
26	27	28	29	30	31	

June

S	M	T	W	T	F	S
						1
2	3	4	5	6	7	8
9	10	11	12	13	14	15
16	17	18	19	20	21	22
23	24	25	26	27	28	29
30						

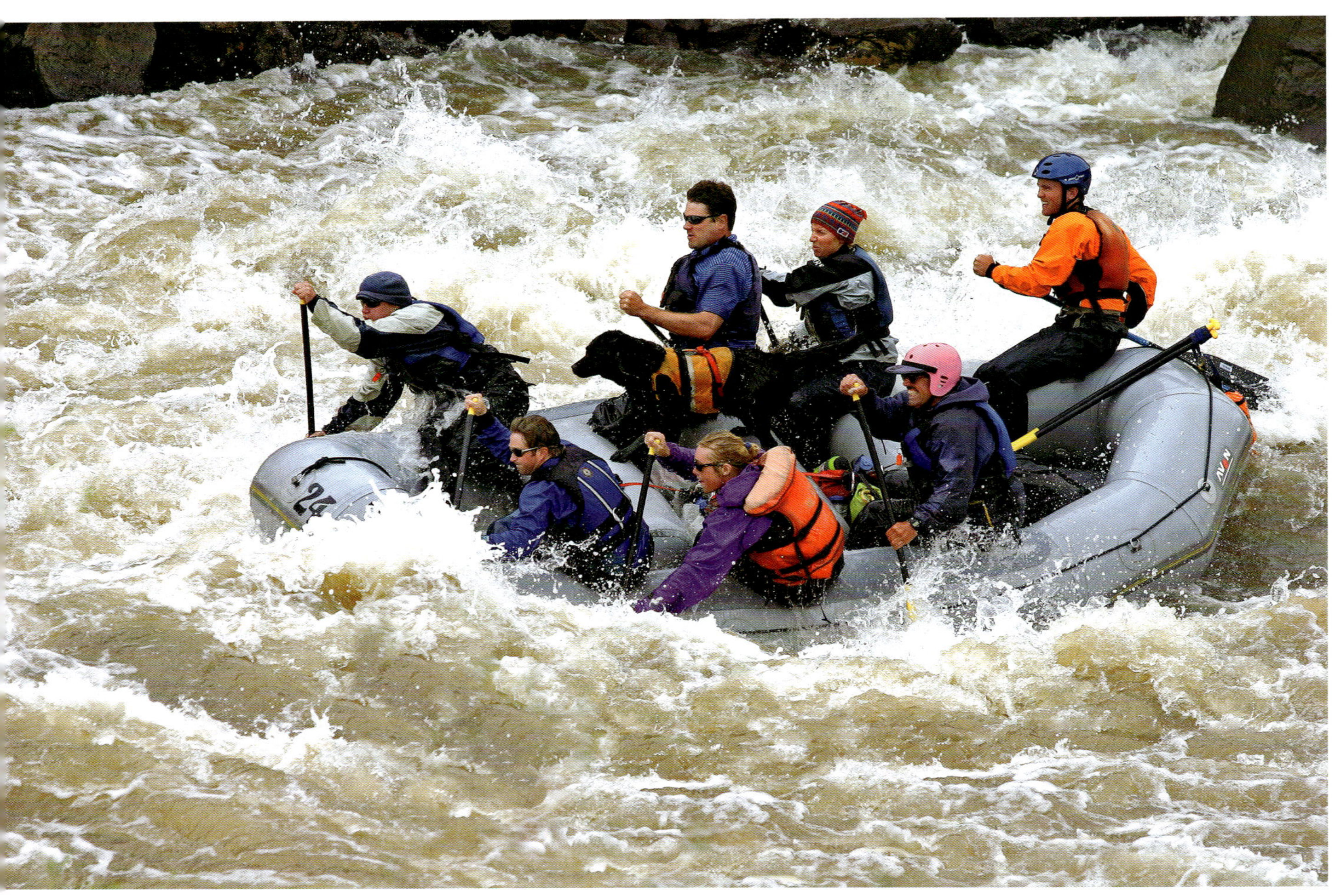

White water rafting on the
Rio Grande, Pilar.

Geraint Smith

May

20 Monday

21 Tuesday

22 Wednesday

23 Thursday

24 Friday

25 Saturday

26 Sunday

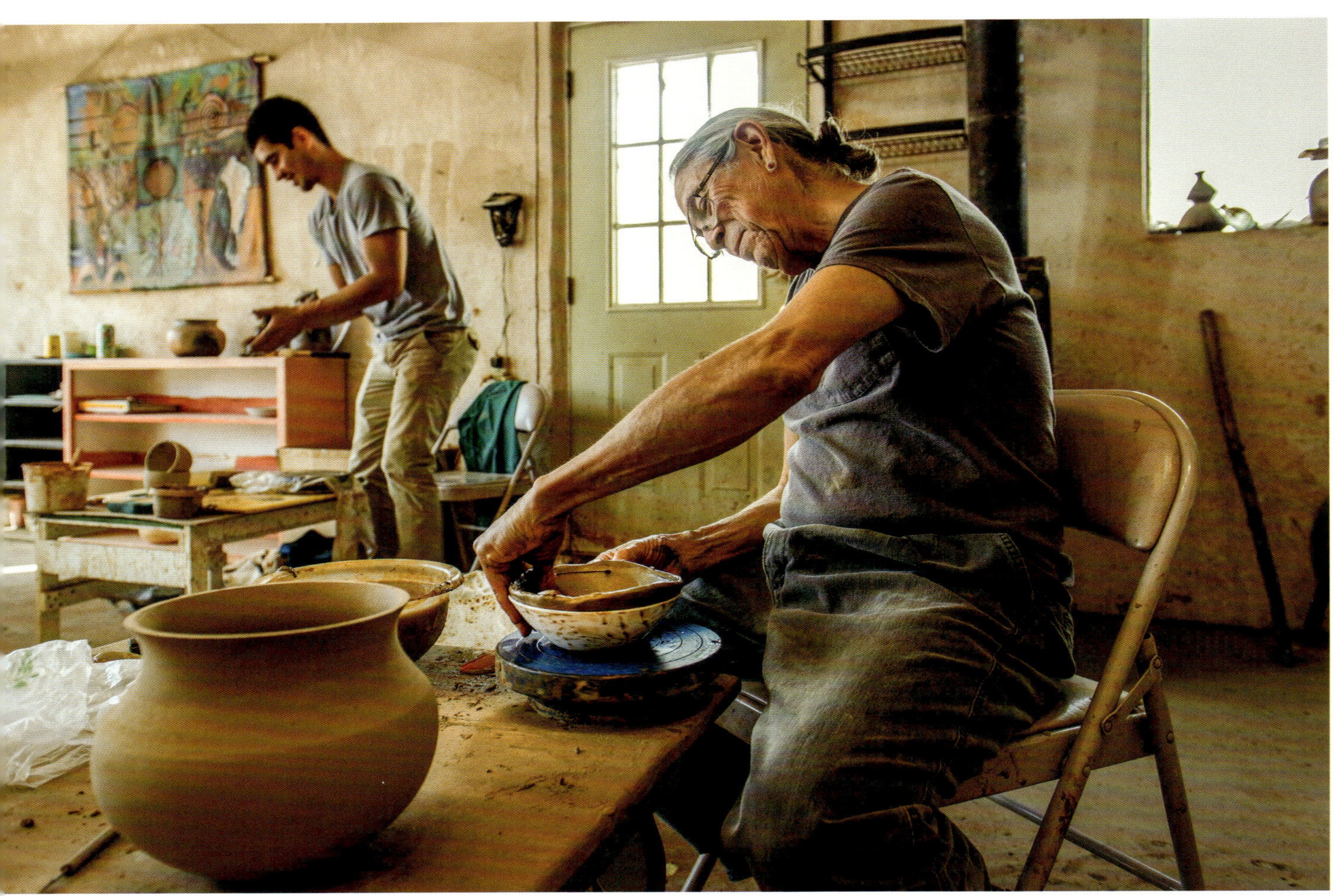

Master potter Felipe Ortega coils a micaceous pot from a self-styled puki, or bowl, that is used as a base in La Madera. His Owl Peak studio welcomed students from all over the world. Ortega passed away in 2018.

Kitty Leaken

Blessing of the Fields and Corn Dance at Tesuque Pueblo, indianpueblo.org/feast-days/

May

27
Monday

Memorial Day

28
Tuesday

29
Wednesday

30
Thursday

◑

31
Friday

June

1
Saturday

LGBTQ+ Pride Month

2
Sunday

May

S	M	T	W	T	F	S
			1	2	3	4
5	6	7	8	9	10	11
12	13	14	15	16	17	18
19	20	21	22	23	24	25
26	27	28	29	30	31	

June

S	M	T	W	T	F	S
						1
2	3	4	5	6	7	8
9	10	11	12	13	14	15
16	17	18	19	20	21	22
23	24	25	26	27	28	29
30						

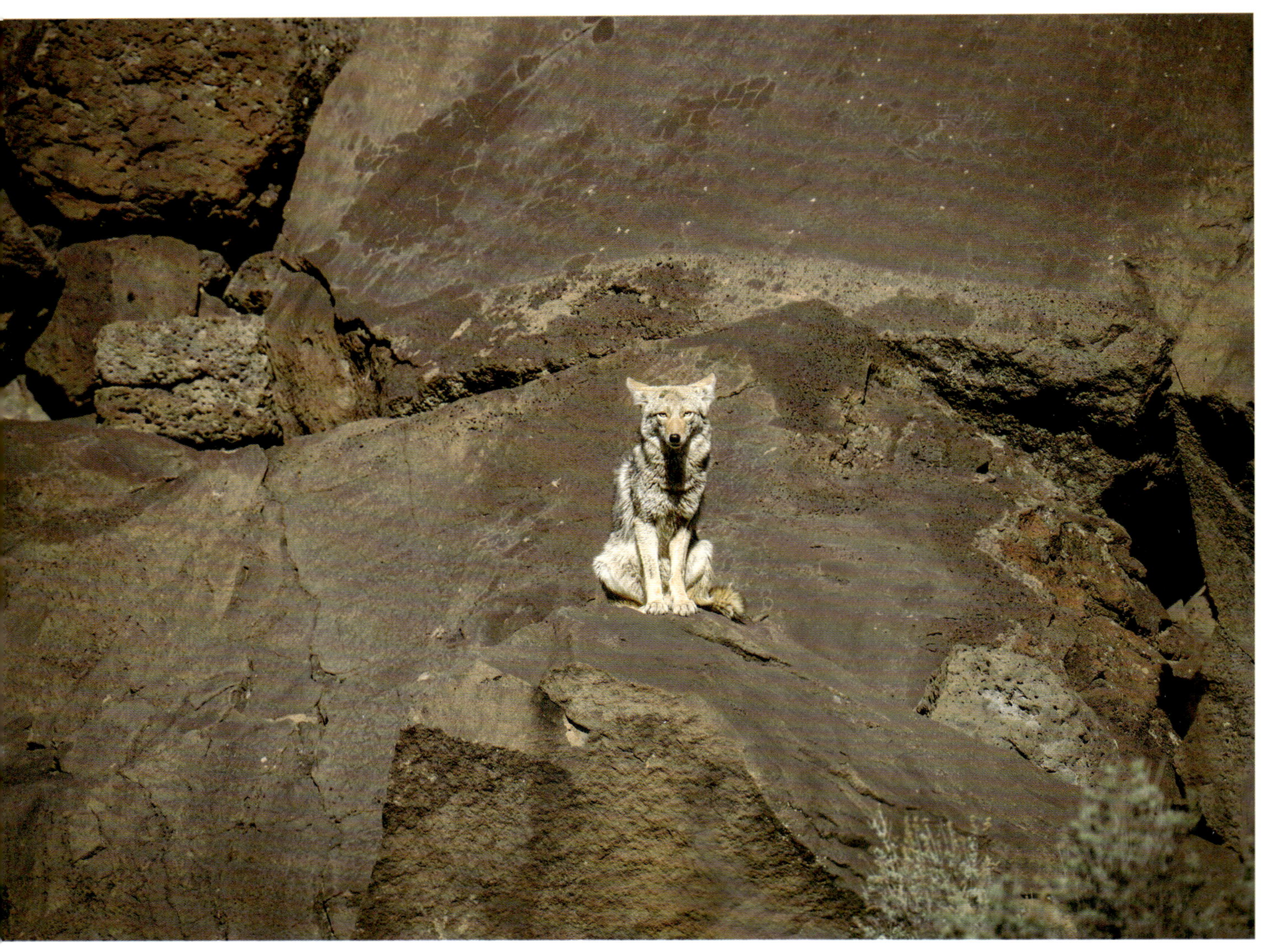

Coyote watches from a large boulder along the Rio Pueblo in the
Rio Grande del Norte National Monument.

Geraint Smith

June

3
Monday

4
Tuesday

5
Wednesday

World Environment Day

6
Thursday

D-Day
●

7
Friday

8
Saturday

9
Sunday

June

S	M	T	W	T	F	S
						1
2	3	4	5	6	7	8
9	10	11	12	13	14	15
16	17	18	19	20	21	22
23	24	25	26	27	28	29
30						

July

S	M	T	W	T	F	S
	1	2	3	4	5	6
7	8	9	10	11	12	13
14	15	16	17	18	19	20
21	22	23	24	25	26	27
28	29	30	31			

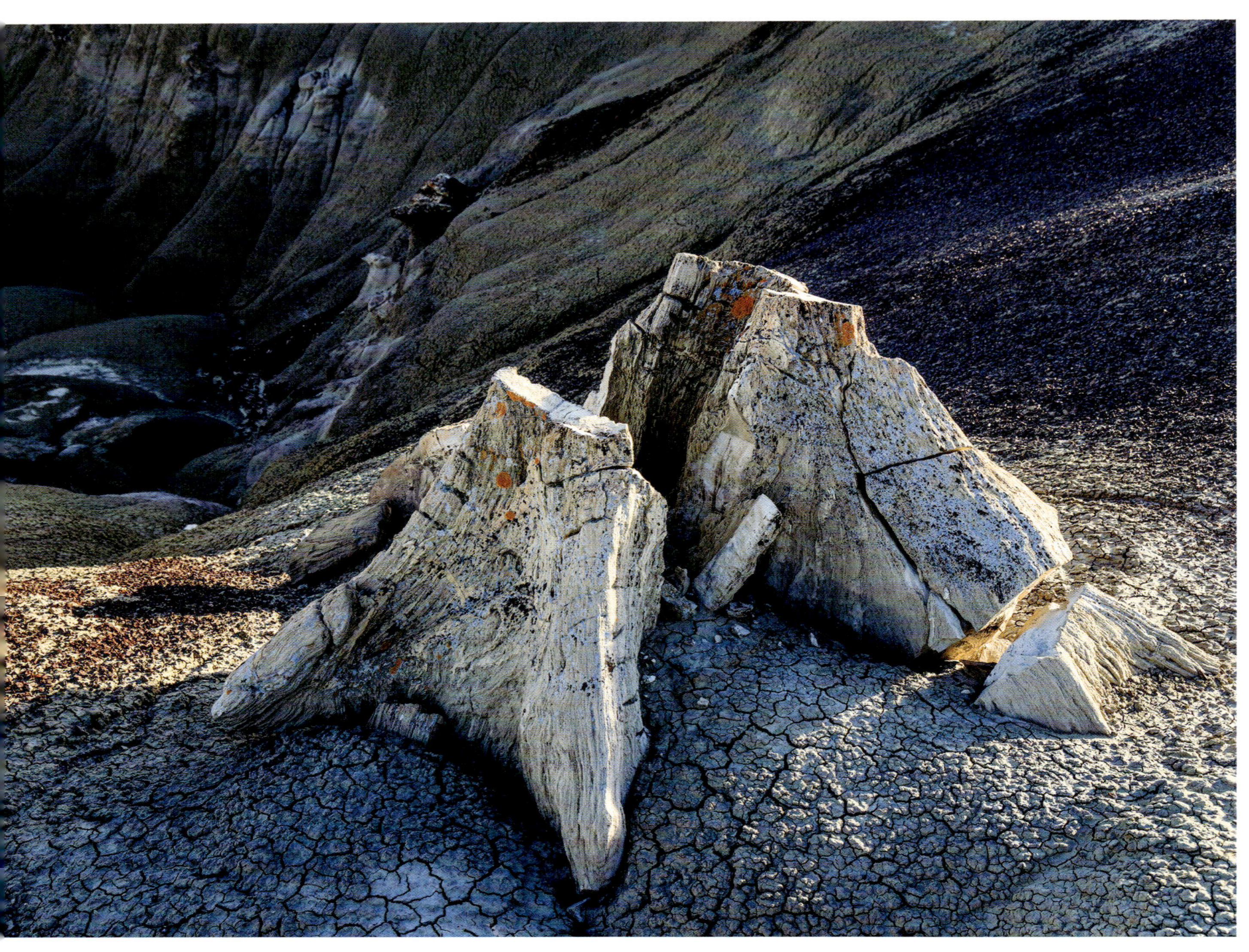

Petrification, San Juan Basin.

Brian VanDenzen

San Antonio Feast Day with various dances at Ohkay Owingeh, Picuris, Sandia, Santa Clara, and Taos Pueblos, indianpueblo.org/feast-days/

June

10
Monday

11
Tuesday

12
Wednesday

13
Thursday

14
Friday

Flag Day

15
Saturday

16
Sunday

Father's Day

June

S	M	T	W	T	F	S
						1
2	3	4	5	6	7	8
9	10	11	12	13	14	15
16	17	18	19	20	21	22
23	24	25	26	27	28	29
30						

July

S	M	T	W	T	F	S
	1	2	3	4	5	6
7	8	9	10	11	12	13
14	15	16	17	18	19	20
21	22	23	24	25	26	27
28	29	30	31			

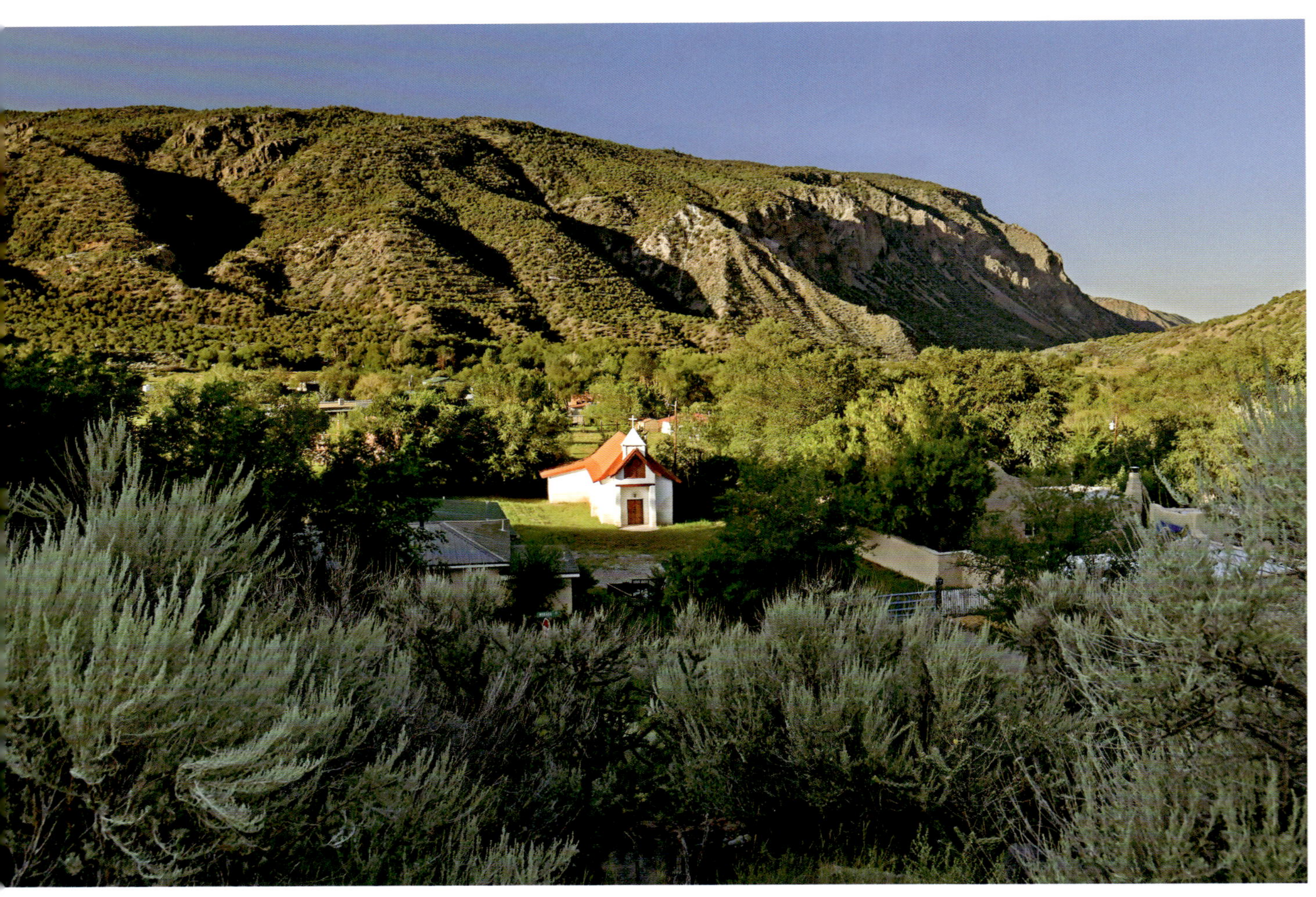

Nuestra Señora de los Dolores Mission
Chapel at sunrise in Pilar.

Gene Peach

Rodeo de Santa Fe at the Santa Fe Rodeo Grounds, rodeodesantafe.org (through June 23)

June						
S	M	T	W	T	F	S
						1
2	3	4	5	6	7	8
9	10	11	12	13	14	15
16	17	18	19	20	21	22
23	24	25	26	27	28	29
30						

July						
S	M	T	W	T	F	S
	1	2	3	4	5	6
7	8	9	10	11	12	13
14	15	16	17	18	19	20
21	22	23	24	25	26	27
28	29	30	31			

June

17
Monday

18
Tuesday

19
Wednesday

Juneteenth

20
Thursday

Summer Solstice

21
Friday

22
Saturday

23
Sunday

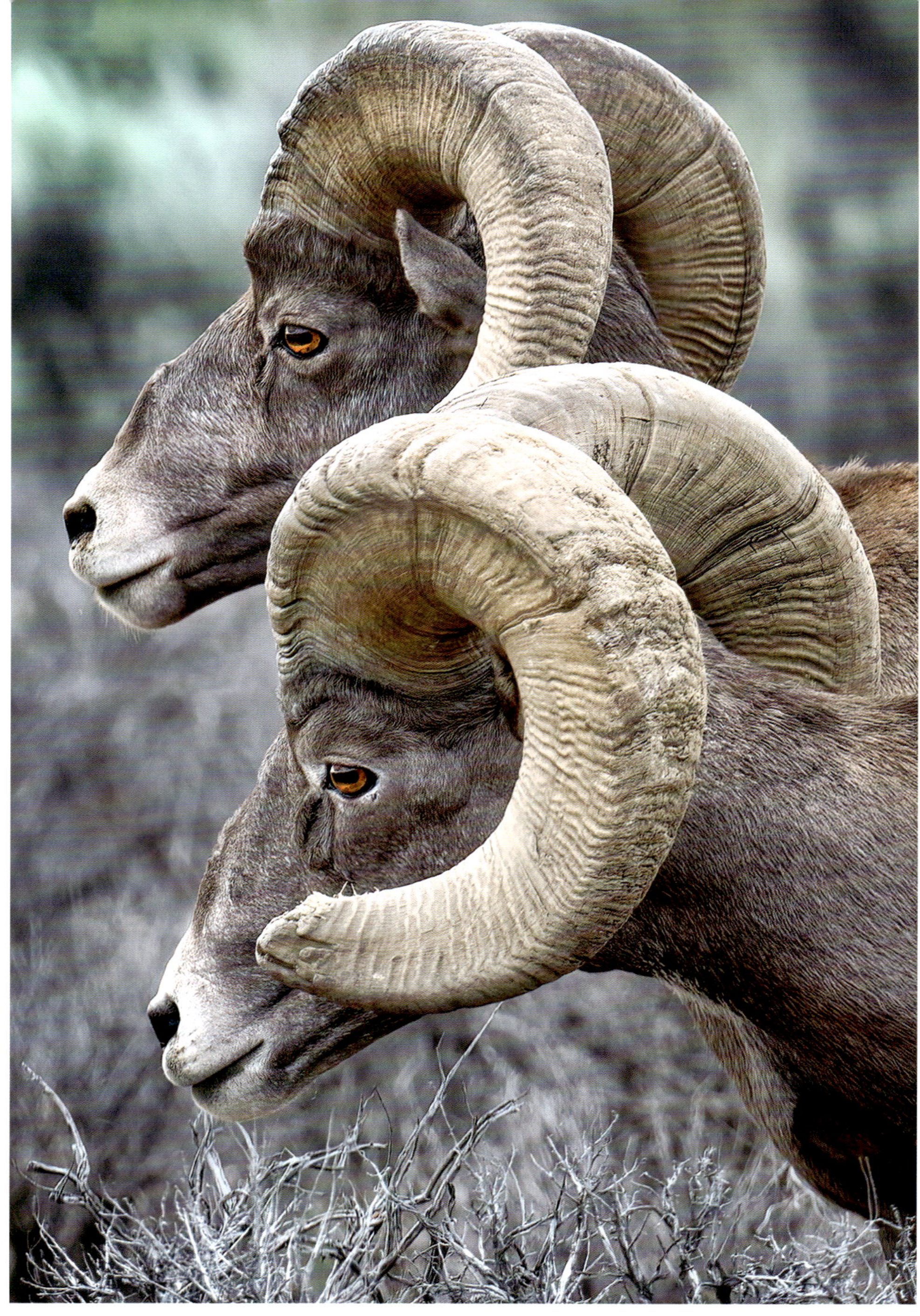

Rocky Mountain
bighorn sheep,
Taos Mesa.

Steven Bundy

June

June

S	M	T	W	T	F	S
						1
2	3	4	5	6	7	8
9	10	11	12	13	14	15
16	17	18	19	20	21	22
23	24	25	26	27	28	29
30						

July

S	M	T	W	T	F	S
	1	2	3	4	5	6
7	8	9	10	11	12	13
14	15	16	17	18	19	20
21	22	23	24	25	26	27
28	29	30	31			

24 Monday

25 Tuesday

26 Wednesday

27 Thursday

28 Friday

29 Saturday

30 Sunday

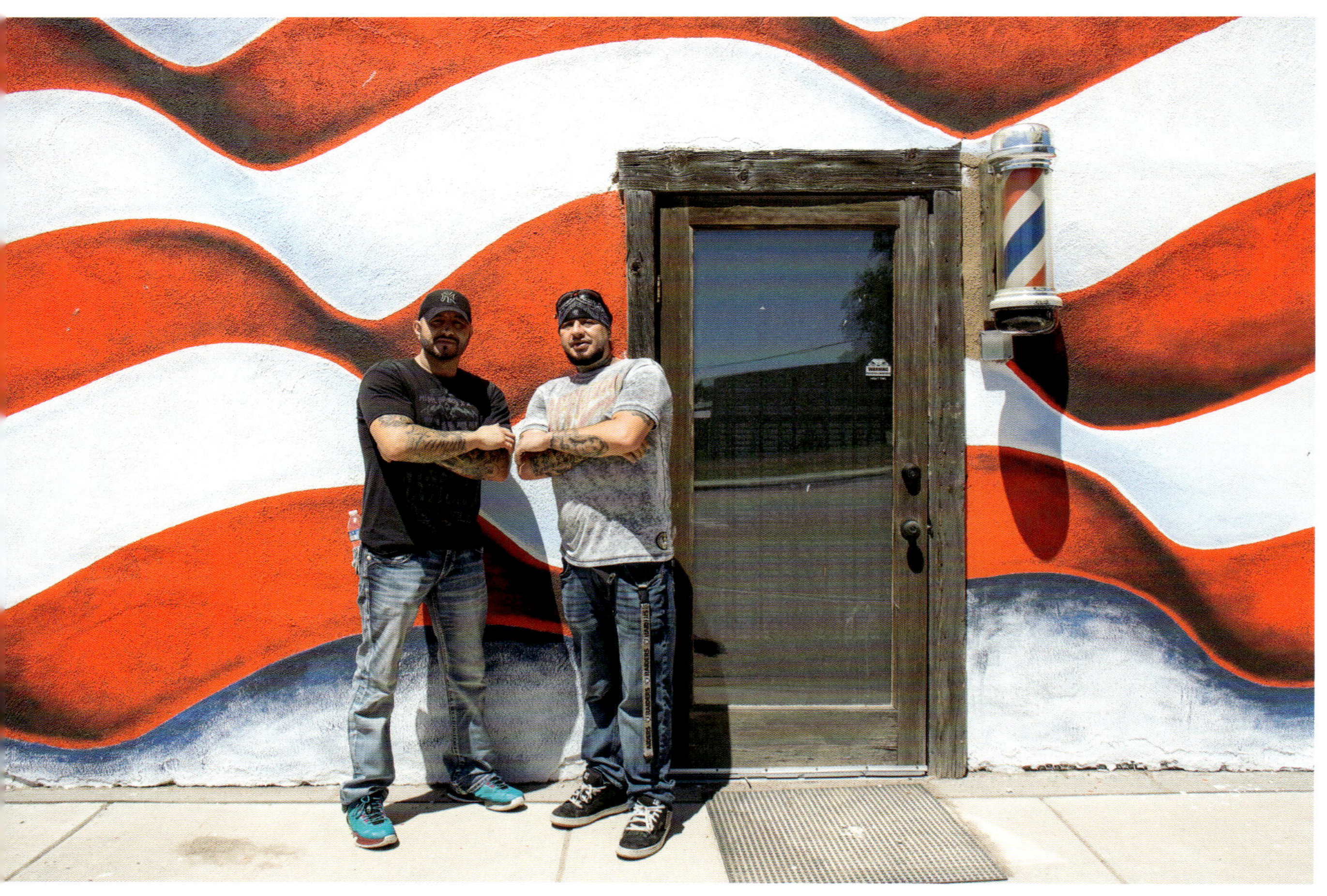

Dominic and Derrick Montoya at their
barbershop in Estancia.

Don J. Usner

July

1
Monday

National Postal Workers Day

2
Tuesday

3
Wednesday

4
Thursday

Independence Day

5
Friday

●

6
Saturday

7
Sunday

July

S	M	T	W	T	F	S
	1	2	3	4	5	6
7	8	9	10	11	12	13
14	15	16	17	18	19	20
21	22	23	24	25	26	27
28	29	30	31			

August

S	M	T	W	T	F	S
				1	2	3
4	5	6	7	8	9	10
11	12	13	14	15	16	17
18	19	20	21	22	23	24
25	26	27	28	29	30	31

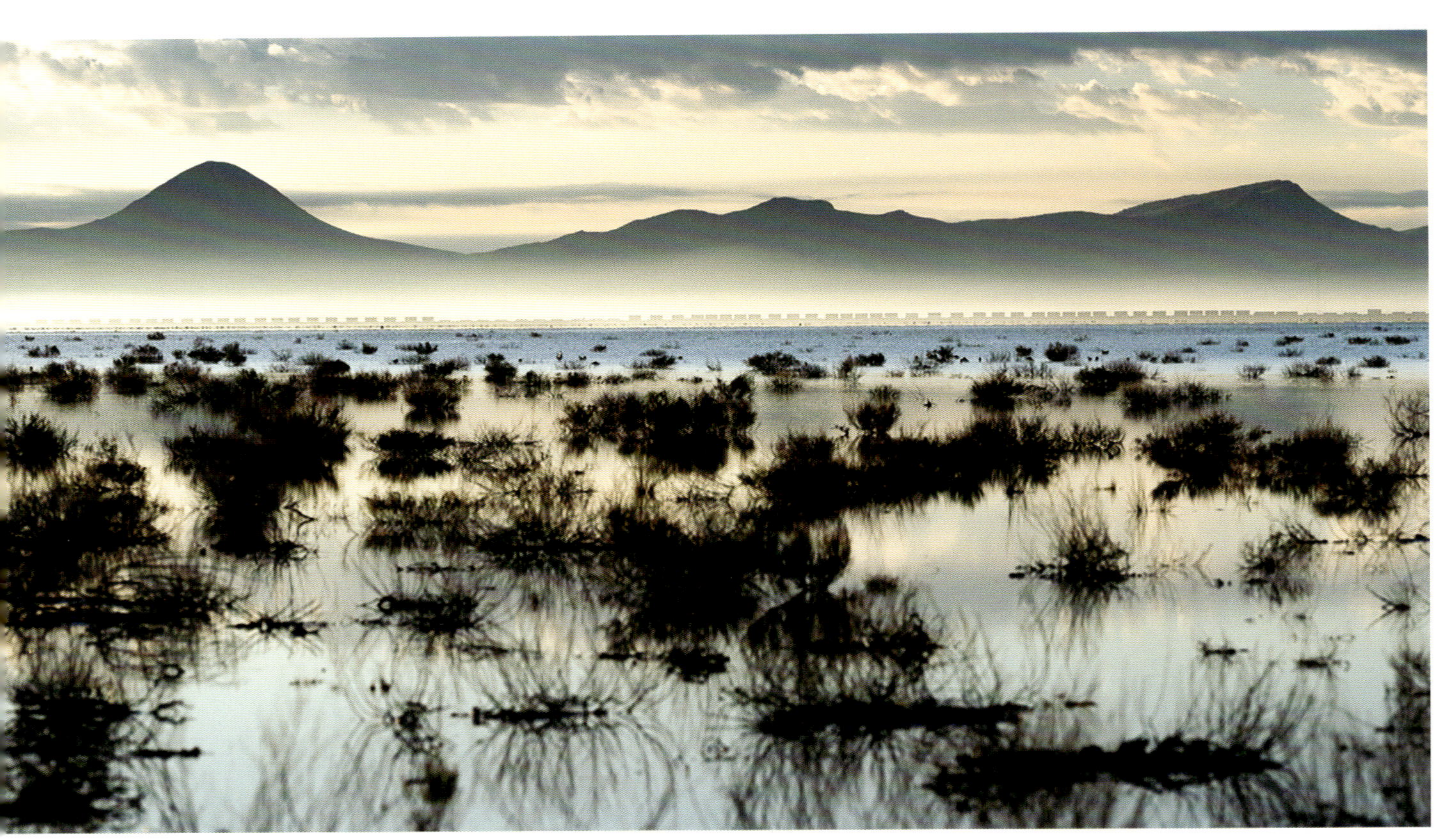

A view across Lordsburg Playa to the train
and highway during the monsoon season.

Esha Chiocchio

July 8   Monday

Silver City CLAY Festival, clayfestival.com (through July 14)

July 12   Friday

Taos Pueblo Pow Wow, taospueblo.com (through July 9)

July 13   Thursday

Los Alamos ScienceFest Discovery Day, losalamossciencefest.com

July 14   Sunday

St. Bonaventure Feast Day with Corn Dance at Cochiti Pueblo, indianpueblo.org/feast-days/

July

S	M	T	W	T	F	S
	1	2	3	4	5	6
7	8	9	10	11	12	13
14	15	16	17	18	19	20
21	22	23	24	25	26	27
28	29	30	31			

August

S	M	T	W	T	F	S
				1	2	3
4	5	6	7	8	9	10
11	12	13	14	15	16	17
18	19	20	21	22	23	24
25	26	27	28	29	30	31

8
Monday

9
Tuesday

10
Wednesday

11
Thursday

12
Friday

13
Saturday

14
Sunday

Bastille Day

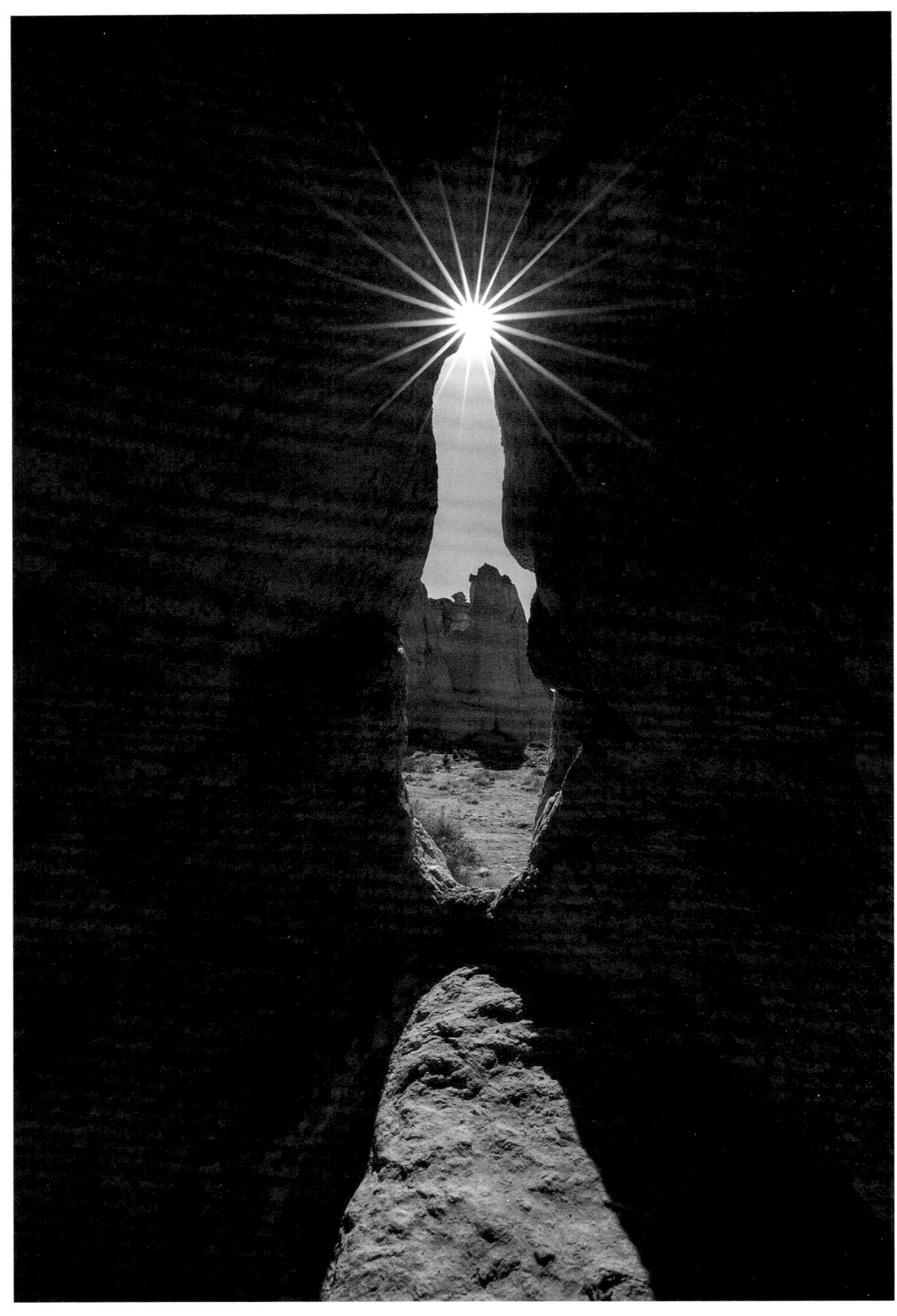

Solstice sunstar, Plaza Blanca.

Geraint Smith

Las Fiestas de Taos, fiestasdetaos.com (through July 21)

July

15
Monday

16
Tuesday

17
Wednesday

18
Thursday

19
Friday

20
Saturday

21
Sunday

July

S	M	T	W	T	F	S
	1	2	3	4	5	6
7	8	9	10	11	12	13
14	15	16	17	18	19	20
21	22	23	24	25	26	27
28	29	30	31			

August

S	M	T	W	T	F	S
				1	2	3
4	5	6	7	8	9	10
11	12	13	14	15	16	17
18	19	20	21	22	23	24
25	26	27	28	29	30	31

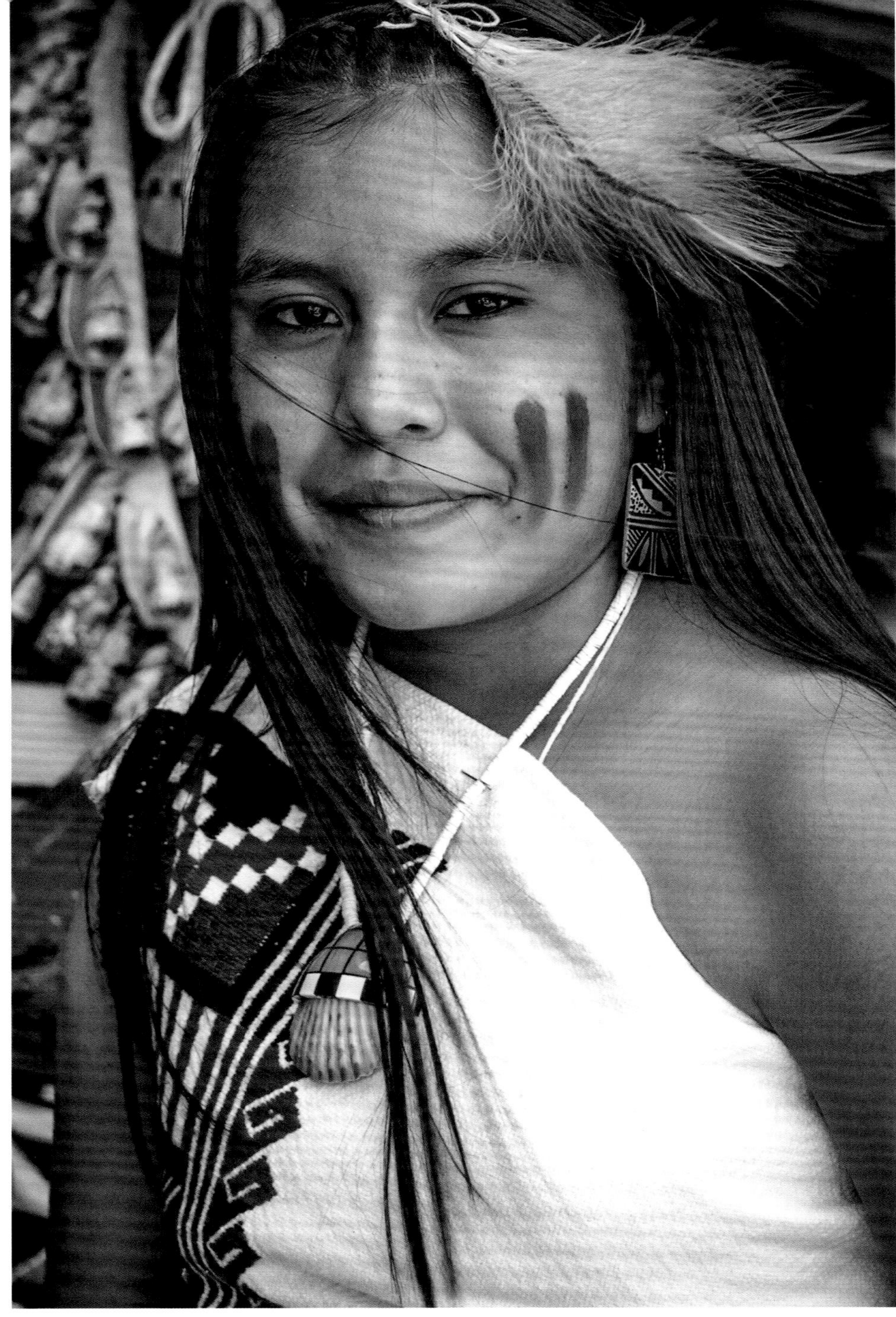

Pueblo dancer, Indian
Pueblo Cultural Center,
Albuquerque.

Jane Whitmore

July

July

S	M	T	W	T	F	S
	1	2	3	4	5	6
7	8	9	10	11	12	13
14	15	16	17	18	19	20
21	22	23	24	25	26	27
28	29	30	31			

August

S	M	T	W	T	F	S
				1	2	3
4	5	6	7	8	9	10
11	12	13	14	15	16	17
18	19	20	21	22	23	24
25	26	27	28	29	30	31

22 Monday

23 Tuesday

24 Wednesday

25 Thursday

26 Friday

National Day of the Cowboy
◐

27 Saturday

Parents' Day

28 Sunday

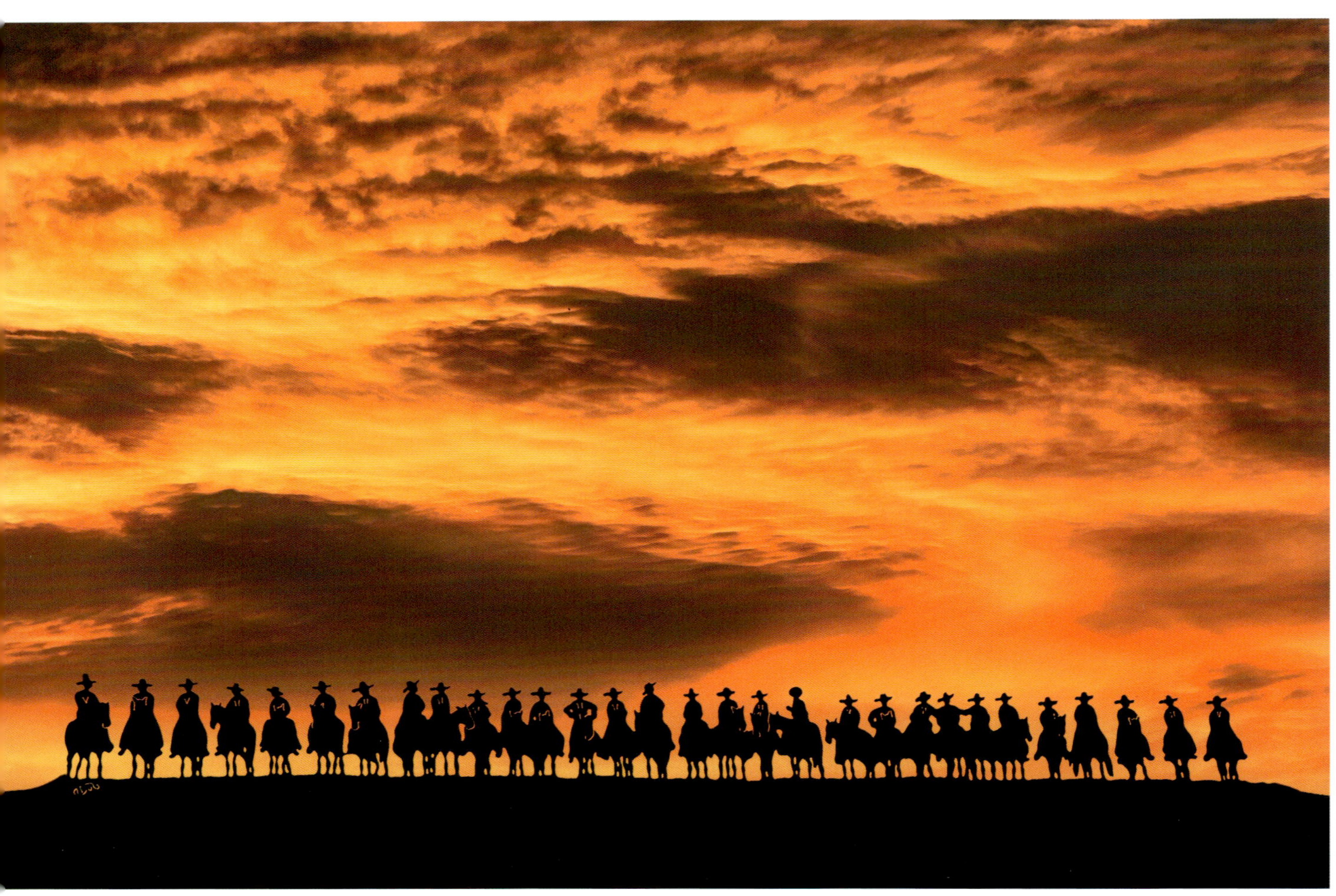

Sculpture on a ranch gate,
Highway 64, Taos.

Geraint Smith

- **Gallup Inter-Tribal Indian Ceremonial**, gallupceremonial.com

- **St. Persingula Feast Day** with Corn Dance at Jemez Pueblo, indianpueblo.org/feast-days/

August 4   Sunday

- **Santo Domingo Feast Day** with Corn Dances at Kewa Pueblo, indianpueblo.org/feast-days/

July

29
Monday

30
Tuesday

International Friendship Day

31
Wednesday

August

1
Thursday

American Artist Appreciation Month

2
Friday

3
Saturday

4
Sunday

July						
S	M	T	W	T	F	S
	1	2	3	4	5	6
7	8	9	10	11	12	13
14	15	16	17	18	19	20
21	22	23	24	25	26	27
28	29	30	31			

August						
S	M	T	W	T	F	S
				1	2	3
4	5	6	7	8	9	10
11	12	13	14	15	16	17
18	19	20	21	22	23	24
25	26	27	28	29	30	31

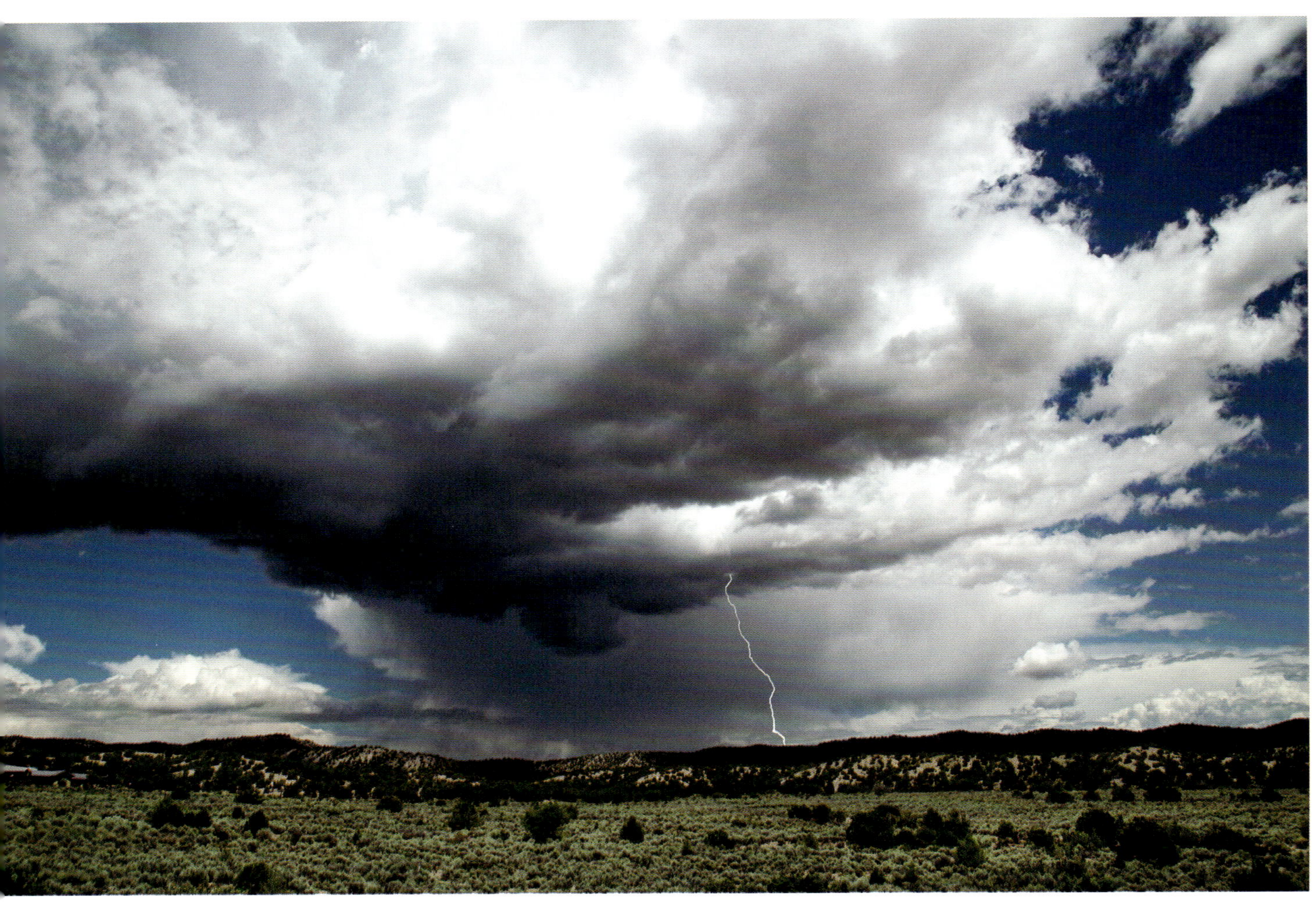

Summer storm, El Rito.

Tom Quinn Kumpf

San Lorenzo Feast Day with ceremonial foot race, pole climb, and traditional dances at Picuris Pueblo, picurispueblo.org; and various dances at Acoma Pueblo, acomaskycity.org

August

August

S	M	T	W	T	F	S
				1	2	3
4	5	6	7	8	9	10
11	12	13	14	15	16	17
18	19	20	21	22	23	24
25	26	27	28	29	30	31

September

S	M	T	W	T	F	S
1	2	3	4	5	6	7
8	9	10	11	12	13	14
15	16	17	18	19	20	21
22	23	24	25	26	27	28
29	30					

5
Monday

6
Tuesday

7
Wednesday

8
Thursday

National Book Lovers Day

9
Friday

Anniversary of 1680 Pueblo Revolt

10
Saturday

11
Sunday

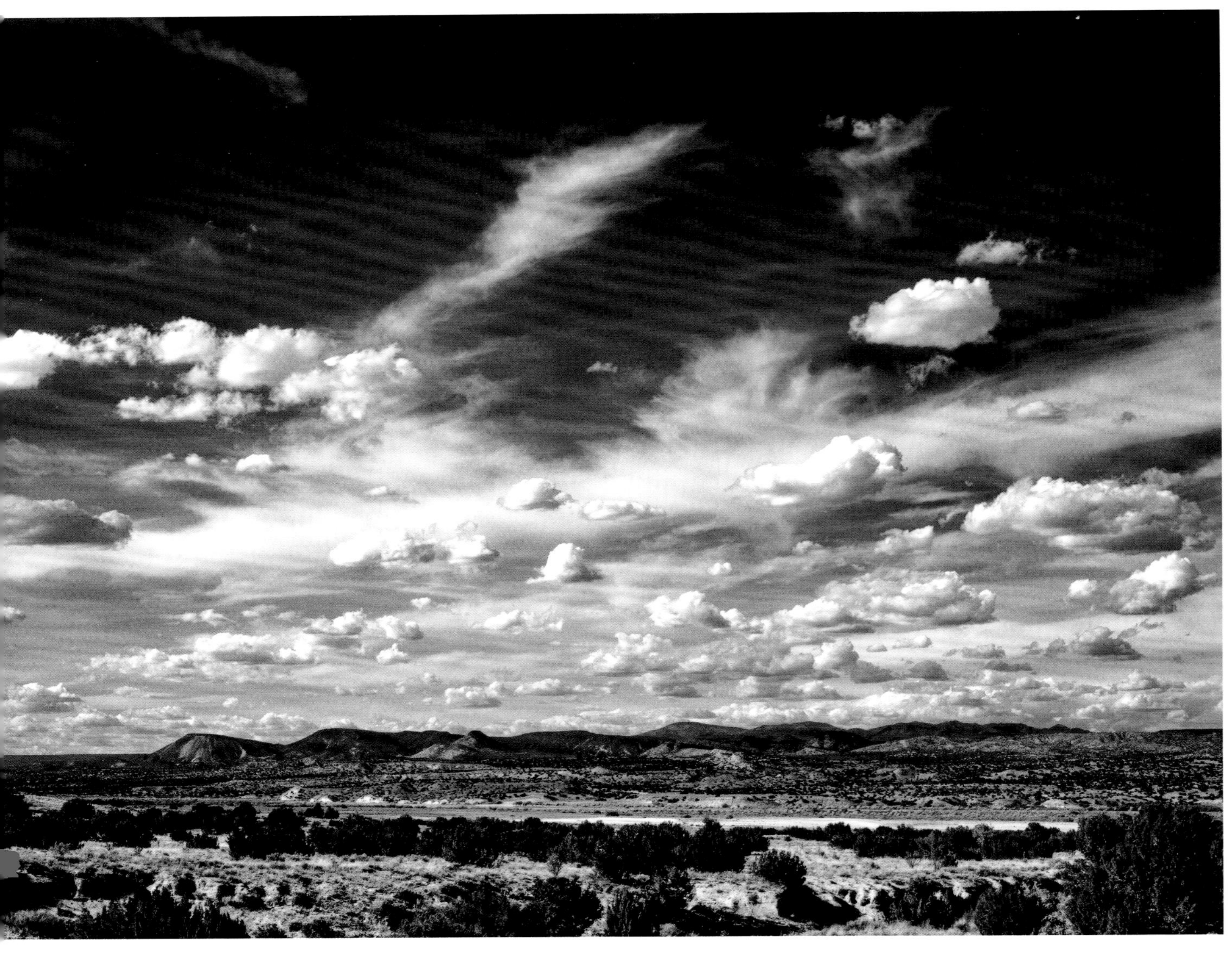

Afternoon summer sky
near Bernalillo.

David Halpern

August 12   Monday

Santa Clara Feast Day with Buffalo, Harvest, and Corn Dances at Santa Clara Pueblo, indianpueblo.org/feast-days/

August 14   Wednesday

Music from Angel Fire Summer Festival, musicfromangelfire.org (through August 28)

August 15   Thursday

Assumption of Our Blessed Mother Feast Day with Corn Dances at Zia Pueblo, zia.com; Harvest and various dances at Laguna Pueblo, lagunapueblo-nsn.gov

August 17   Saturday

Santa Fe Indian Market on the Santa Fe Plaza, swaia.org (through August 18)

August

August						
S	M	T	W	T	F	S
				1	2	3
4	5	6	7	8	9	10
11	12	13	14	15	16	17
18	19	20	21	22	23	24
25	26	27	28	29	30	31

September						
S	M	T	W	T	F	S
1	2	3	4	5	6	7
8	9	10	11	12	13	14
15	16	17	18	19	20	21
22	23	24	25	26	27	28
29	30					

12 Monday

◐

13 Tuesday

14 Wednesday

National Navajo Code Talkers Day

15 Thursday

16 Friday

17 Saturday

18 Sunday

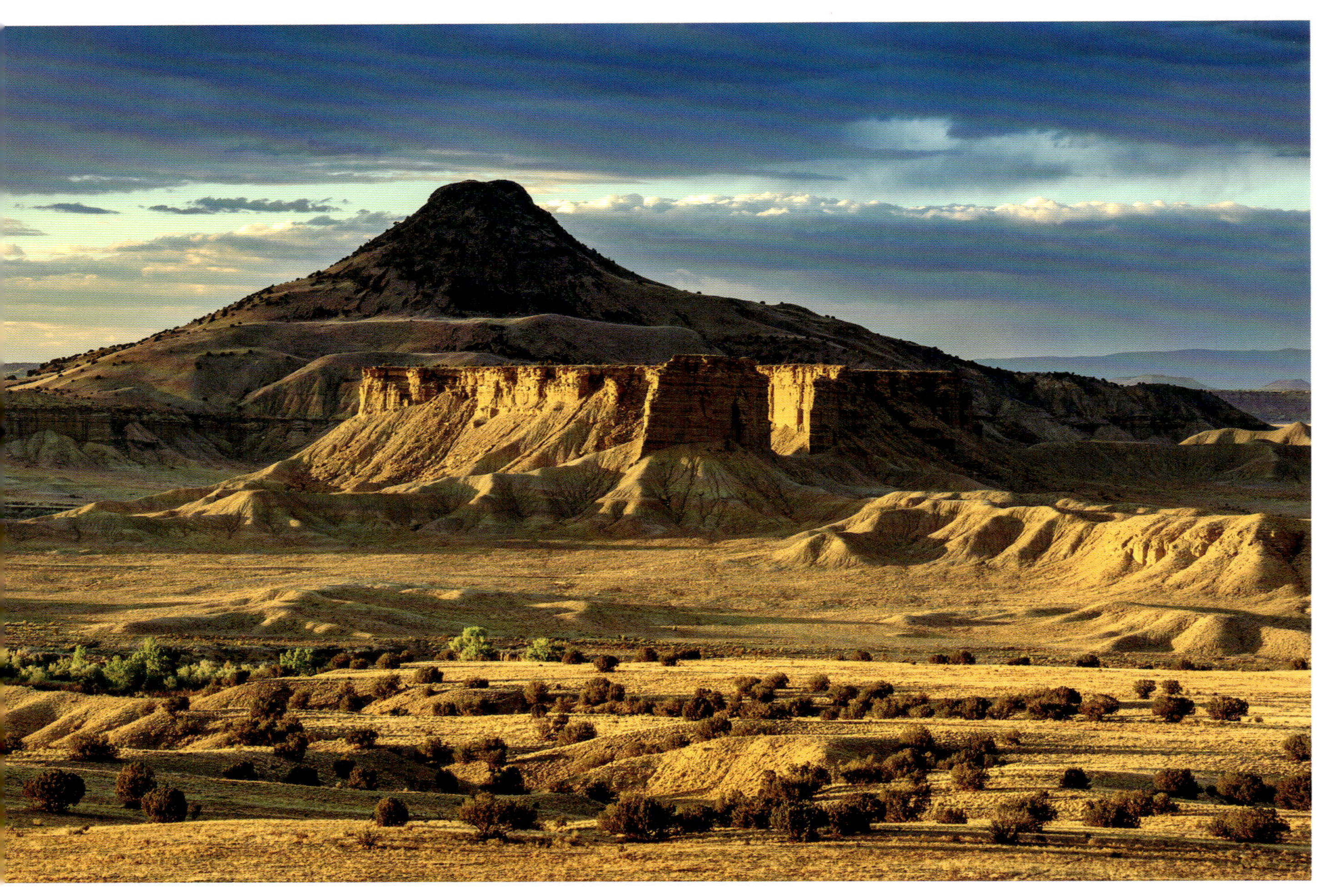

Photograph of Cerro Cuate taken late on a
summer's day in the Rio Puerco Valley.

David Cushman

Great American Duck Race in Deming,
demingduckrace.com

August

August

19
Monday

20
Tuesday

Senior Citizens Day

21
Wednesday

22
Thursday

23
Friday

24
Saturday

25
Sunday

August

S	M	T	W	T	F	S
				1	2	3
4	5	6	7	8	9	10
11	12	13	14	15	16	17
18	19	20	21	22	23	24
25	26	27	28	29	30	31

September

S	M	T	W	T	F	S
1	2	3	4	5	6	7
8	9	10	11	12	13	14
15	16	17	18	19	20	21
22	23	24	25	26	27	28
29	30					

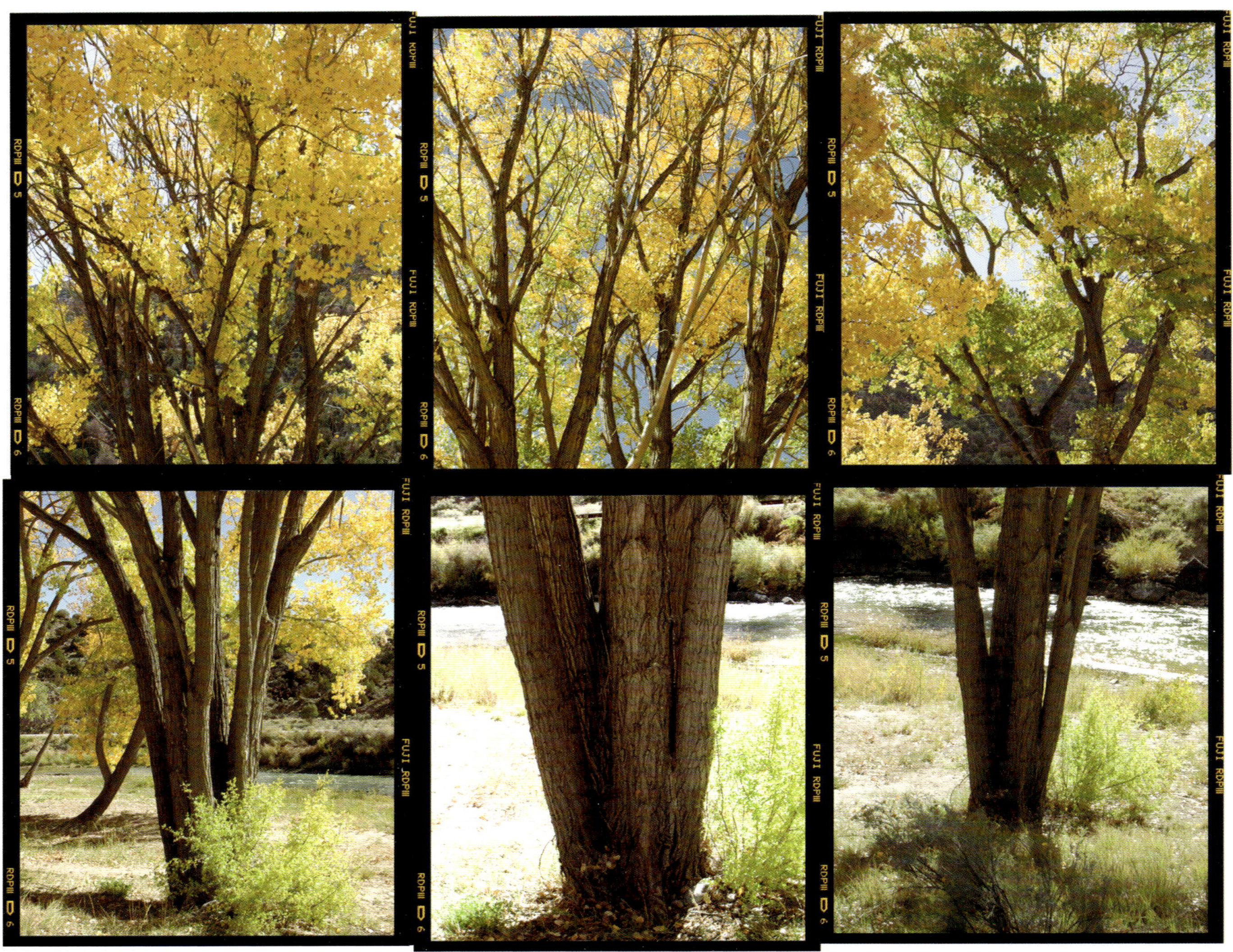

Cottonwood trees by the
Galisteo Creek in Galisteo.

Peter Ogilvie

August

August						
S	M	T	W	T	F	S
				1	2	3
4	5	6	7	8	9	10
11	12	13	14	15	16	17
18	19	20	21	22	23	24
25	26	27	28	29	30	31

September						
S	M	T	W	T	F	S
1	2	3	4	5	6	7
8	9	10	11	12	13	14
15	16	17	18	19	20	21
22	23	24	25	26	27	28
29	30					

Women's Equality Day

26 Monday

27 Tuesday

28 Wednesday

29 Thursday

30 Friday

31 Saturday

September

1 Sunday

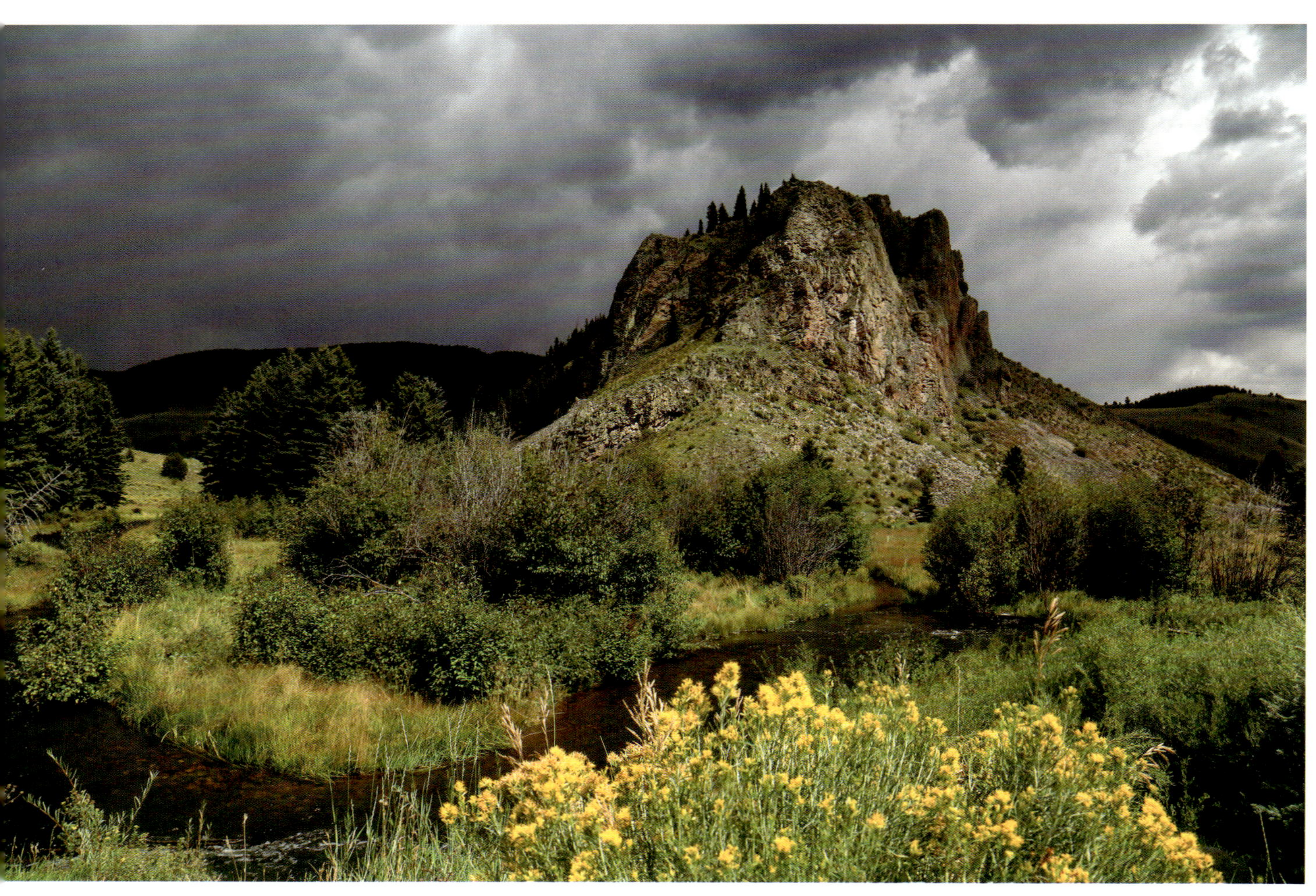

Comanche Point, on the
way to Valle Vidal.

Bill Curry

September

San Esteban Feast Day with Harvest Dance at Acoma Pueblo, indianpueblo.org/feast-days/

Fiesta de Santa Fe, santafefiesta.org (through September 16)

Nativity of the Blessed Virgin Feast Day with Harvest and Social Dances at Village of Encinal, Laguna Pueblo, lagunapueblo-nsn.gov

September

S	M	T	W	T	F	S
1	2	3	4	5	6	7
8	9	10	11	12	13	14
15	16	17	18	19	20	21
22	23	24	25	26	27	28
29	30					

October

S	M	T	W	T	F	S
		1	2	3	4	5
6	7	8	9	10	11	12
13	14	15	16	17	18	19
20	21	22	23	24	25	26
27	28	29	30	31		

2 Monday

Labor Day
●

3 Tuesday

4 Wednesday

National Wildlife Day

5 Thursday

6 Friday

National Read a Book Day

7 Saturday

8 Sunday

International Literacy Day
National Grandparents' Day

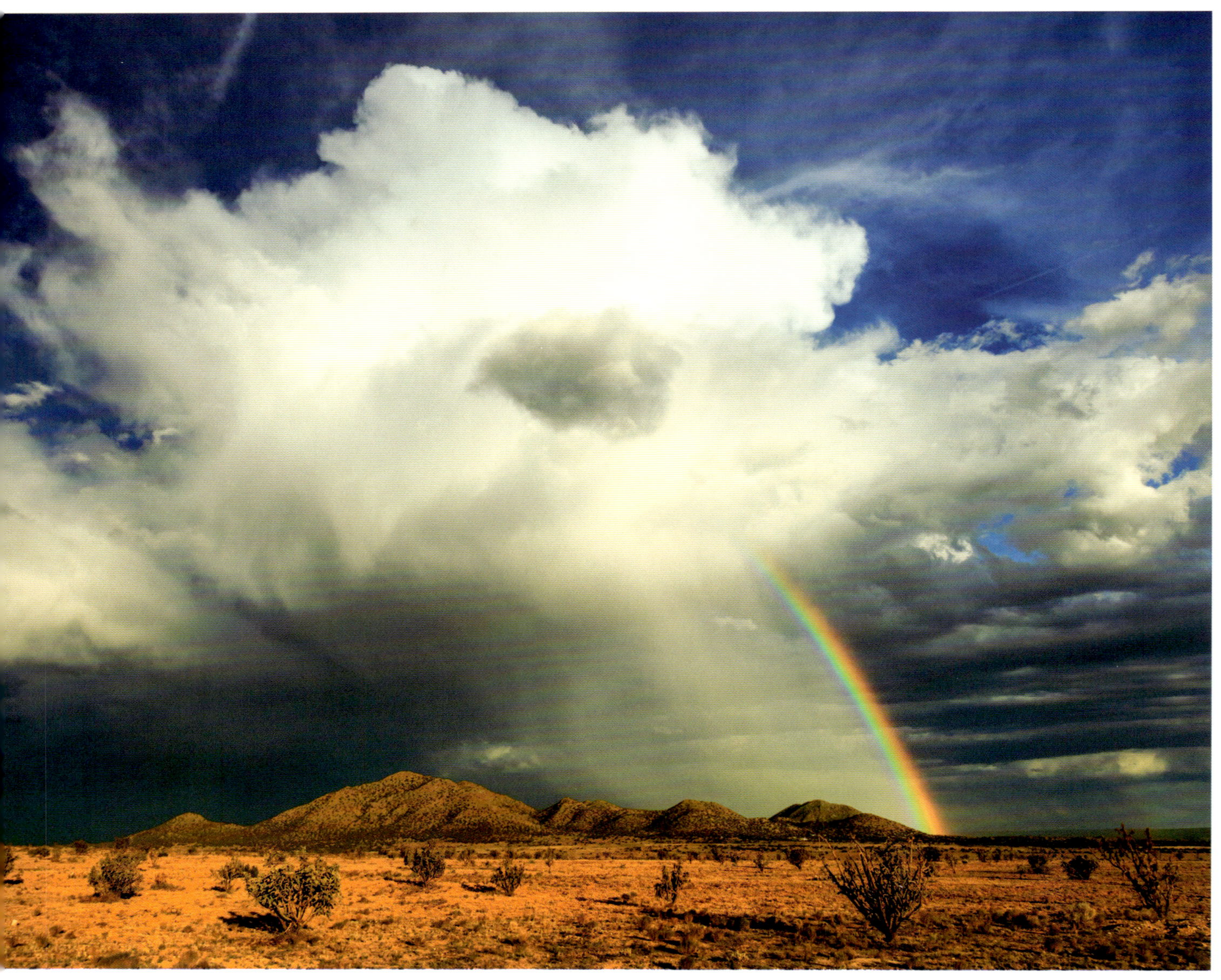

Monsoon rainbow, Cerrillos Hills,
Santa Fe County.

Brian VanDenzen

New Mexico State Fair begins,
Albuquerque, statefair.exponm.com
(through September 22)

September

9
Monday

10
Tuesday

◑

11
Wednesday

Patriot Day

12
Thursday

13
Friday

14
Saturday

15
Sunday

National Hispanic Heritage Month (through October 15)

September

S	M	T	W	T	F	S
1	2	3	4	5	6	7
8	9	10	11	12	13	14
15	16	17	18	19	20	21
22	23	24	25	26	27	28
29	30					

October

S	M	T	W	T	F	S
		1	2	3	4	5
6	7	8	9	10	11	12
13	14	15	16	17	18	19
20	21	22	23	24	25	26
27	28	29	30	31		

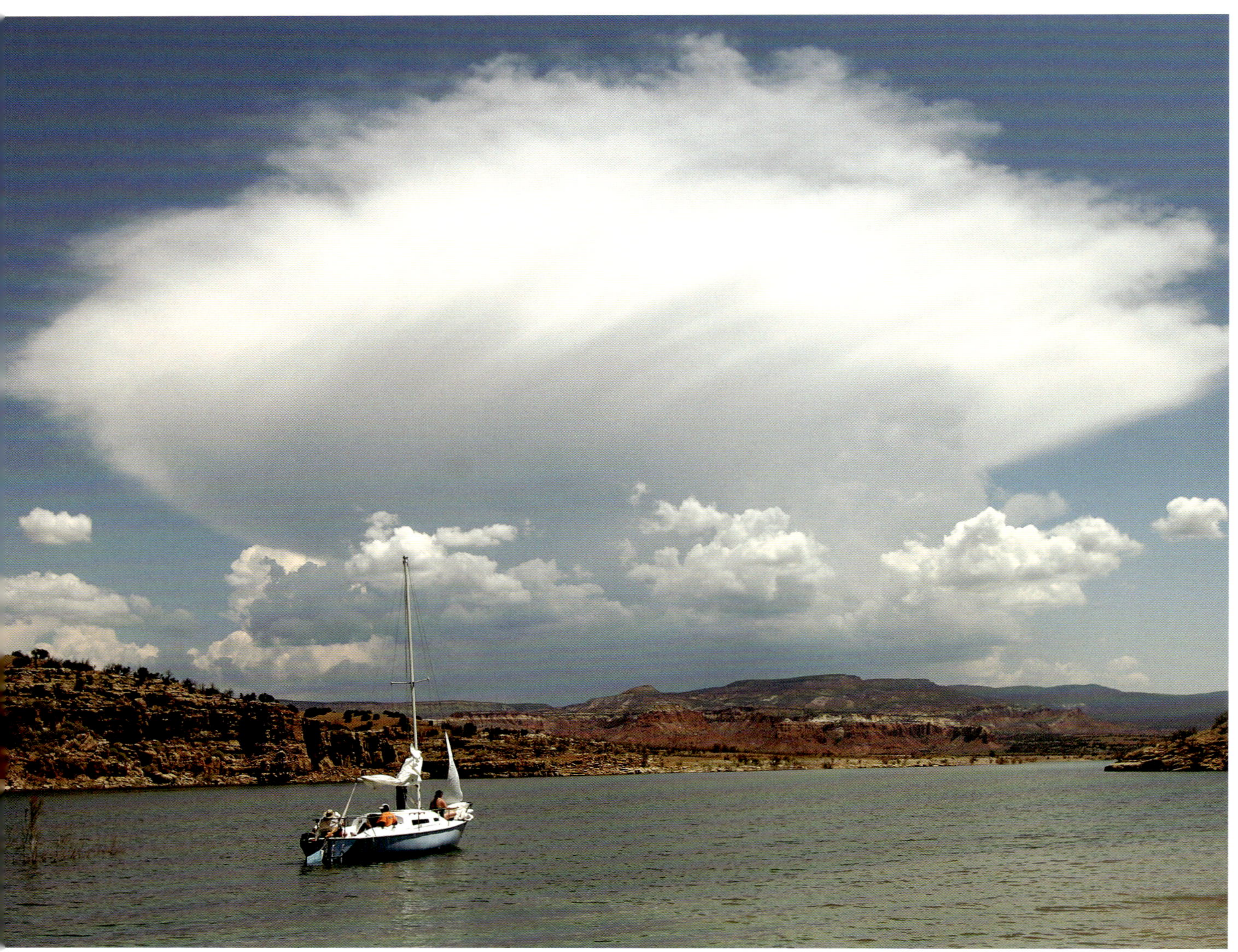

Preparing to set sail on Abiquiu Lake.

Bob Felice

September

16
Monday

17
Tuesday

18
Wednesday

19
Thursday

20
Friday

21
Saturday

22
Sunday

Autumnal Equinox

September

S	M	T	W	T	F	S
1	2	3	4	5	6	7
8	9	10	11	12	13	14
15	16	17	18	19	20	21
22	23	24	25	26	27	28
29	30					

October

S	M	T	W	T	F	S
		1	2	3	4	5
6	7	8	9	10	11	12
13	14	15	16	17	18	19
20	21	22	23	24	25	26
27	28	29	30	31		

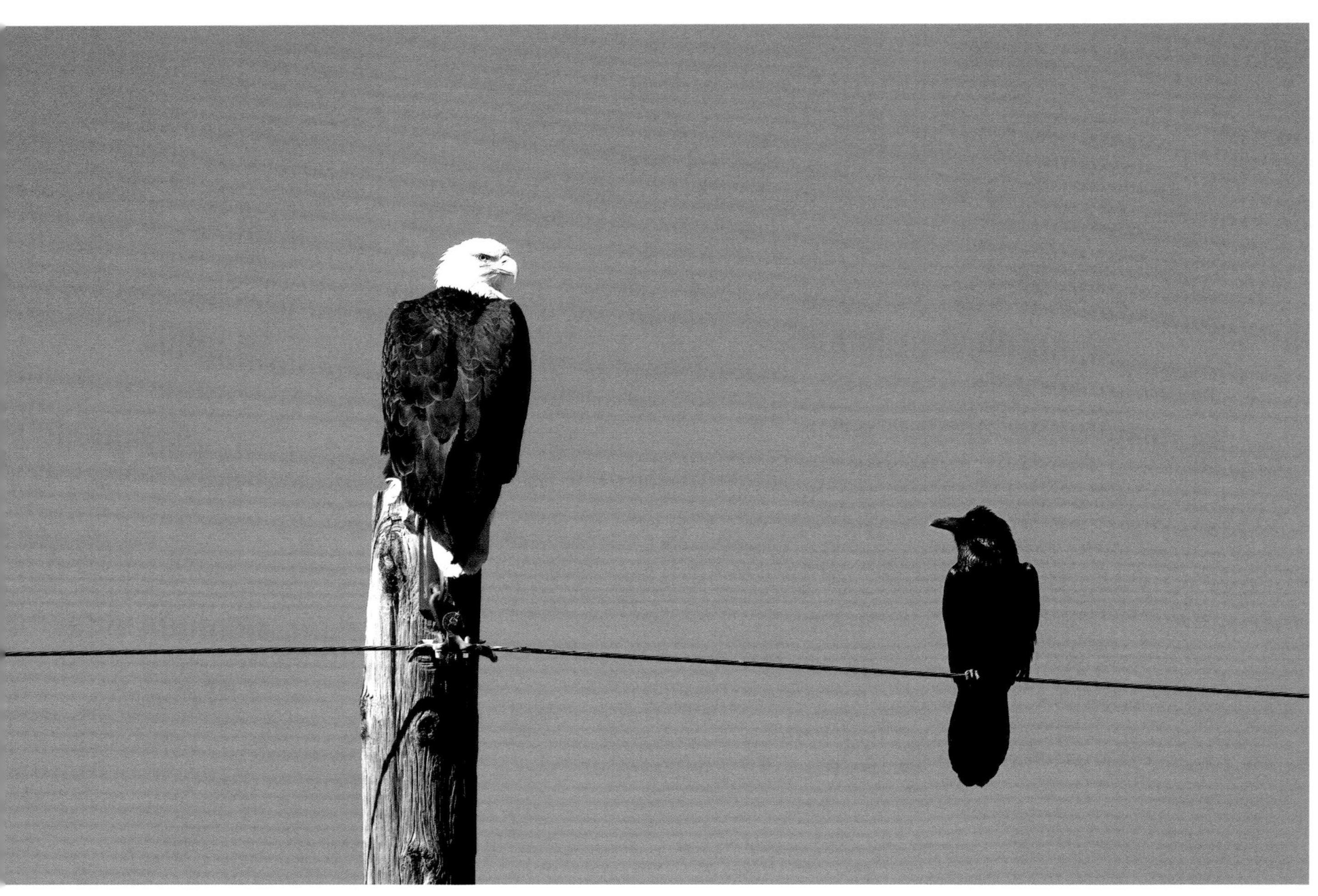

A bald eagle and raven hold a conversation in Costilla.

Geraint Smith

September 25   Wednesday

St. Elizabeth Feast Day with Harvest Dance and other various dances at Paguate Village, Laguna Pueblo, lagunapueblo-nsn.gov

Southern New Mexico State Fair & Rodeo in Las Cruces, snmstatefairgrounds.net (through September 29)

September 27   Friday

All American CowboyFest at Ruidoso, allamericancowboyfest.com (through September 29)

September 30   Saturday

San Geronimo Feast Day with arts and crafts fair, foot races, and pole climb at Taos Pueblo, taospueblo.com

September

S	M	T	W	T	F	S
1	2	3	4	5	6	7
8	9	10	11	12	13	14
15	16	17	18	19	20	21
22	23	24	25	26	27	28
29	30					

October

S	M	T	W	T	F	S
		1	2	3	4	5
6	7	8	9	10	11	12
13	14	15	16	17	18	19
20	21	22	23	24	25	26
27	28	29	30	31		

23
Monday

Yom Kippur (begins sundown September 24 and ends nightfall September 25)

24
Tuesday

25
Wednesday

26
Thursday

27
Friday

28
Saturday

National Public Lands Day

29
Sunday

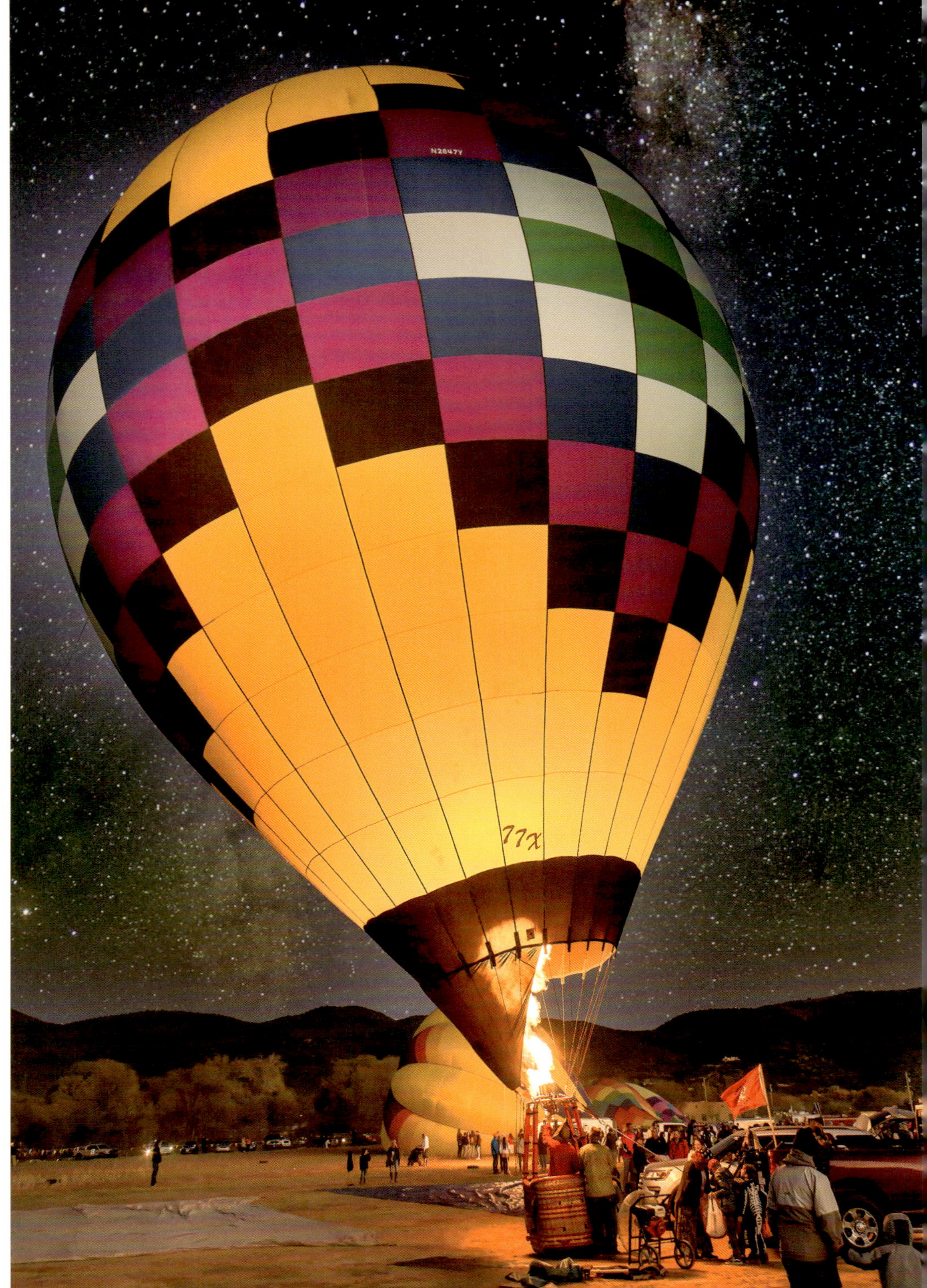

Taos Balloon Fiesta.

Steven Bundy

October 4   Friday

● **St. Francis of Assisi Feast Day** with various dances at Nambé Pueblo, nambepueblo.org

October 5   Saturday

● **Albuquerque International Balloon Fiesta** at Balloon Fiesta Park, balloonfiesta.com (through October 13)

● **Mountain and Valley Wool Festival in Santa Fe**, wavwawoolfest.org (through October 6)

September

30
Monday

October

1
Tuesday

National Arts & Humanities Month
International Music Day

2
Wednesday

Rosh Hashanah (begins sundown today and ends nightfall October 4)
●

3
Thursday

4
Friday

5
Saturday

6
Sunday

September

S	M	T	W	T	F	S
1	2	3	4	5	6	7
8	9	10	11	12	13	14
15	16	17	18	19	20	21
22	23	24	25	26	27	28
29	30					

October

S	M	T	W	T	F	S
		1	2	3	4	5
6	7	8	9	10	11	12
13	14	15	16	17	18	19
20	21	22	23	24	25	26
27	28	29	30	31		

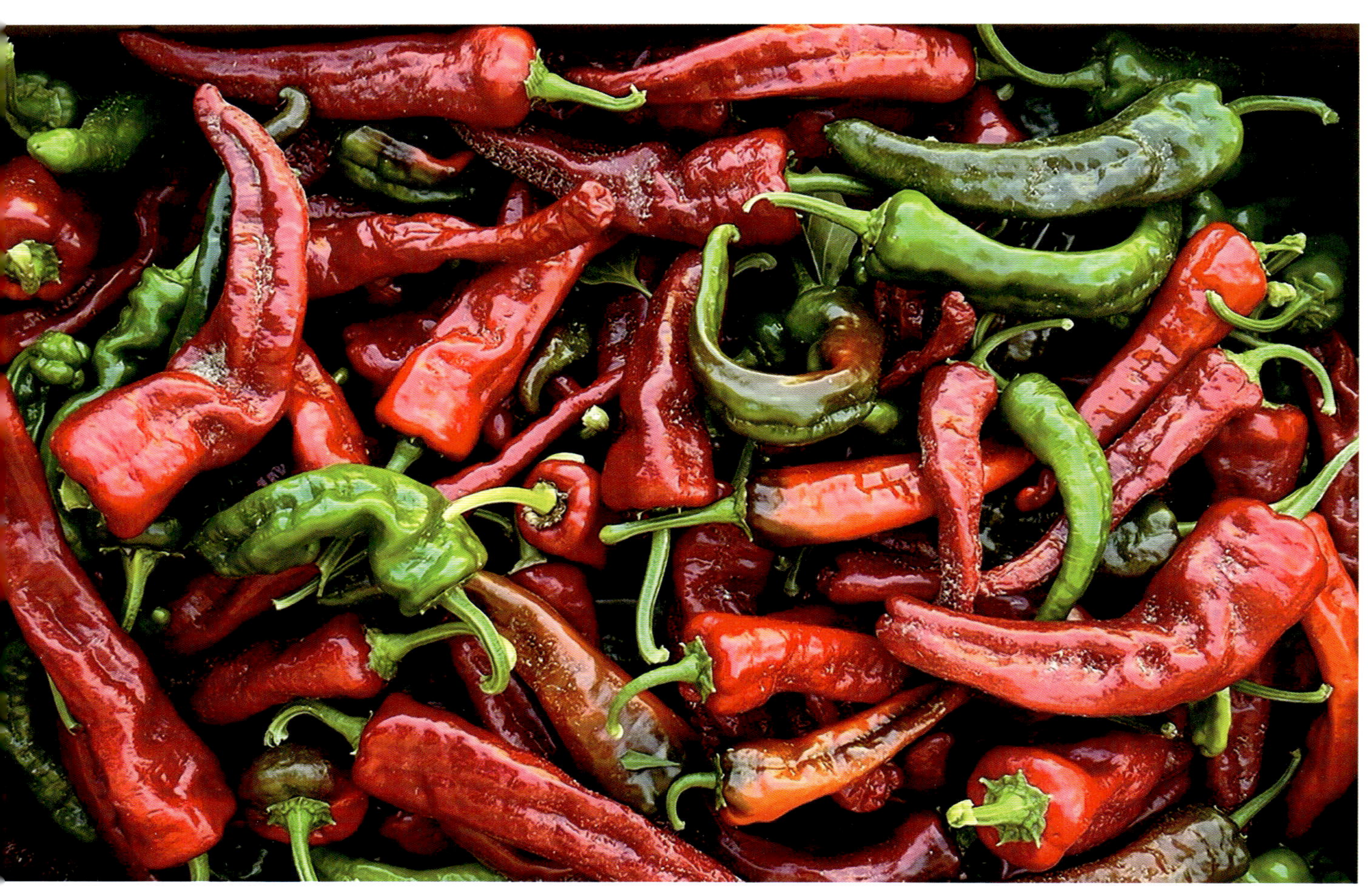

A fresh harvest of red and
green chile, Chimayó.

Fred Wilbur

Santa Fe International Film Festival, santafe.film (through October 13)

October

Child Health Day

7
Monday

8
Tuesday

Indigenous Peoples' Day

9
Wednesday

◑

10
Thursday

Yom Kippur (begins sundown today and ends nightfall October 12)

11
Friday

12
Saturday

13
Sunday

October

S	M	T	W	T	F	S
			1	2	3	4	5
6	7	8	9	10	11	12
13	14	15	16	17	18	19
20	21	22	23	24	25	26
27	28	29	30	31		

November

S	M	T	W	T	F	S
					1	2
3	4	5	6	7	8	9
10	11	12	13	14	15	16
17	18	19	20	21	22	23
24	25	26	27	28	29	30

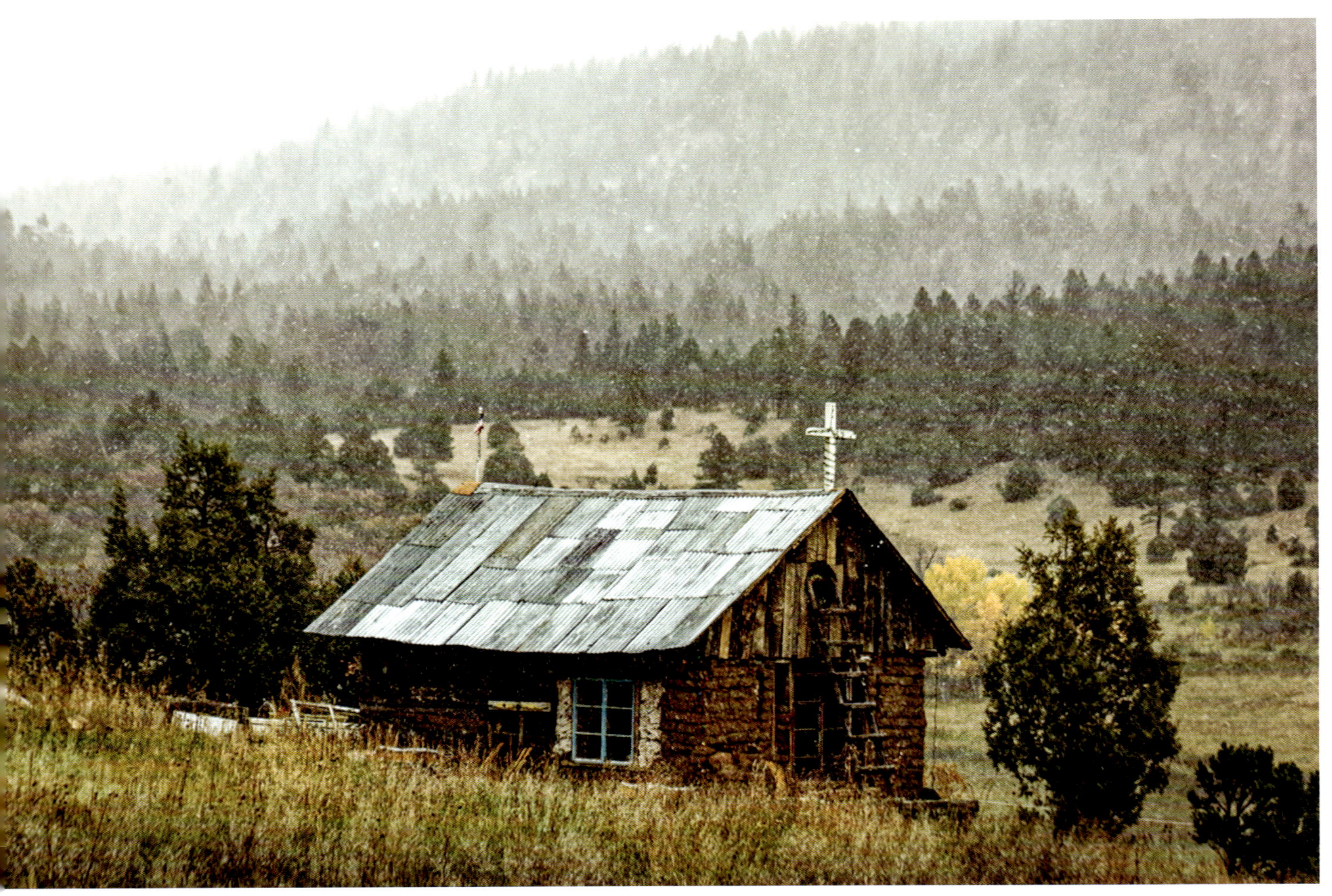

Nestled between the Cristo and Rincon Mountains
in Mora County. Winter storms start in early fall
in El Valle de los Borregos..

Robert Brewer

St. Margaret Mary Feast Day
with Harvest Dance and various
other dances at Laguna Pueblo,
lagunapueblo-nsn.gov

October

14
Monday

15
Tuesday

16
Wednesday

Boss's Day

17
Thursday

Black Poetry Day
○

18
Friday

19
Saturday

20
Sunday

October

S	M	T	W	T	F	S
		1	2	3	4	5
6	7	8	9	10	11	12
13	14	15	16	17	18	19
20	21	22	23	24	25	26
27	28	29	30	31		

November

S	M	T	W	T	F	S
					1	2
3	4	5	6	7	8	9
10	11	12	13	14	15	16
17	18	19	20	21	22	23
24	25	26	27	28	29	30

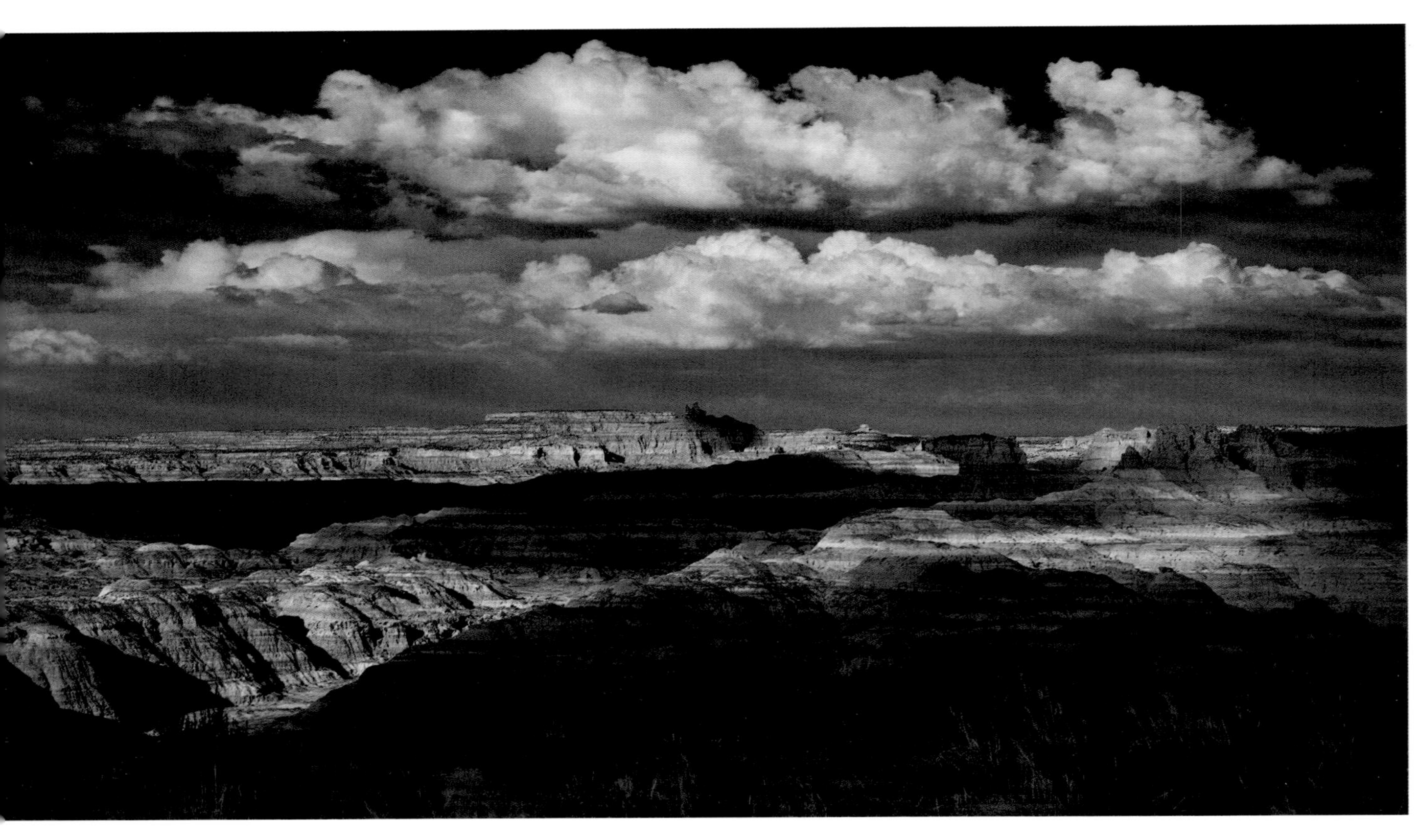

Twin Angels Peak.

Kirk Gittings

October 21   Monday

Southwest Word Fiesta, Silver City, www.swwordfiesta.org (through October 27)

October 25   Friday

Taos Mountain Balloon Rally, taosballoonrally.com (through October 27)

21
Monday

22
Tuesday

23
Wednesday

United Nations Day
◑

24
Thursday

International Artist's Day

25
Friday

26
Saturday

27
Sunday

October

S	M	T	W	T	F	S
		1	2	3	4	5
6	7	8	9	10	11	12
13	14	15	16	17	18	19
20	21	22	23	24	25	26
27	28	29	30	31		

November

S	M	T	W	T	F	S
					1	2
3	4	5	6	7	8	9
10	11	12	13	14	15	16
17	18	19	20	21	22	23
24	25	26	27	28	29	30

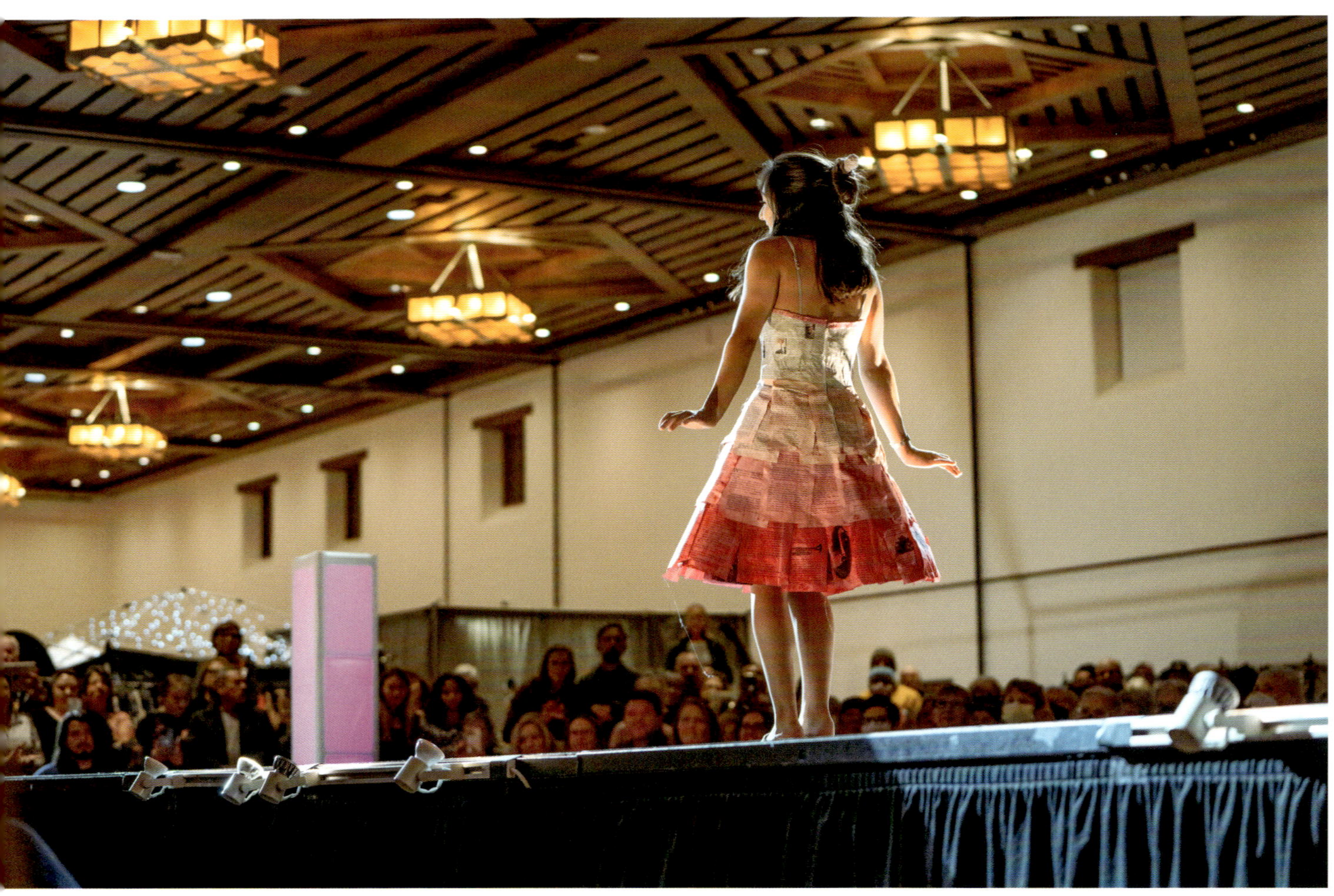

A local student models a custom dress made
from recycled materials on the runway at the
Recycle Santa Fe Art Fashion Show.

Zubin Stillings

October

28
Monday

29
Tuesday

30
Wednesday

31
Thursday

Halloween

November

All Saints Day
American Indian Heritage Month
National Family Stories Month
National Authors Day
●

1
Friday

All Souls Day
Día de los Muertos/Day of the Dead

2
Saturday

Daylight Saving Time ends

3
Sunday

<table>
<tr><td colspan="7">October</td></tr>
<tr><td>S</td><td>M</td><td>T</td><td>W</td><td>T</td><td>F</td><td>S</td></tr>
<tr><td></td><td></td><td>1</td><td>2</td><td>3</td><td>4</td><td>5</td></tr>
<tr><td>6</td><td>7</td><td>8</td><td>9</td><td>10</td><td>11</td><td>12</td></tr>
<tr><td>13</td><td>14</td><td>15</td><td>16</td><td>17</td><td>18</td><td>19</td></tr>
<tr><td>20</td><td>21</td><td>22</td><td>23</td><td>24</td><td>25</td><td>26</td></tr>
<tr><td>27</td><td>28</td><td>29</td><td>30</td><td>31</td><td></td><td></td></tr>
</table>

<table>
<tr><td colspan="7">November</td></tr>
<tr><td>S</td><td>M</td><td>T</td><td>W</td><td>T</td><td>F</td><td>S</td></tr>
<tr><td></td><td></td><td></td><td></td><td></td><td>1</td><td>2</td></tr>
<tr><td>3</td><td>4</td><td>5</td><td>6</td><td>7</td><td>8</td><td>9</td></tr>
<tr><td>10</td><td>11</td><td>12</td><td>13</td><td>14</td><td>15</td><td>16</td></tr>
<tr><td>17</td><td>18</td><td>19</td><td>20</td><td>21</td><td>22</td><td>23</td></tr>
<tr><td>24</td><td>25</td><td>26</td><td>27</td><td>28</td><td>29</td><td>30</td></tr>
</table>

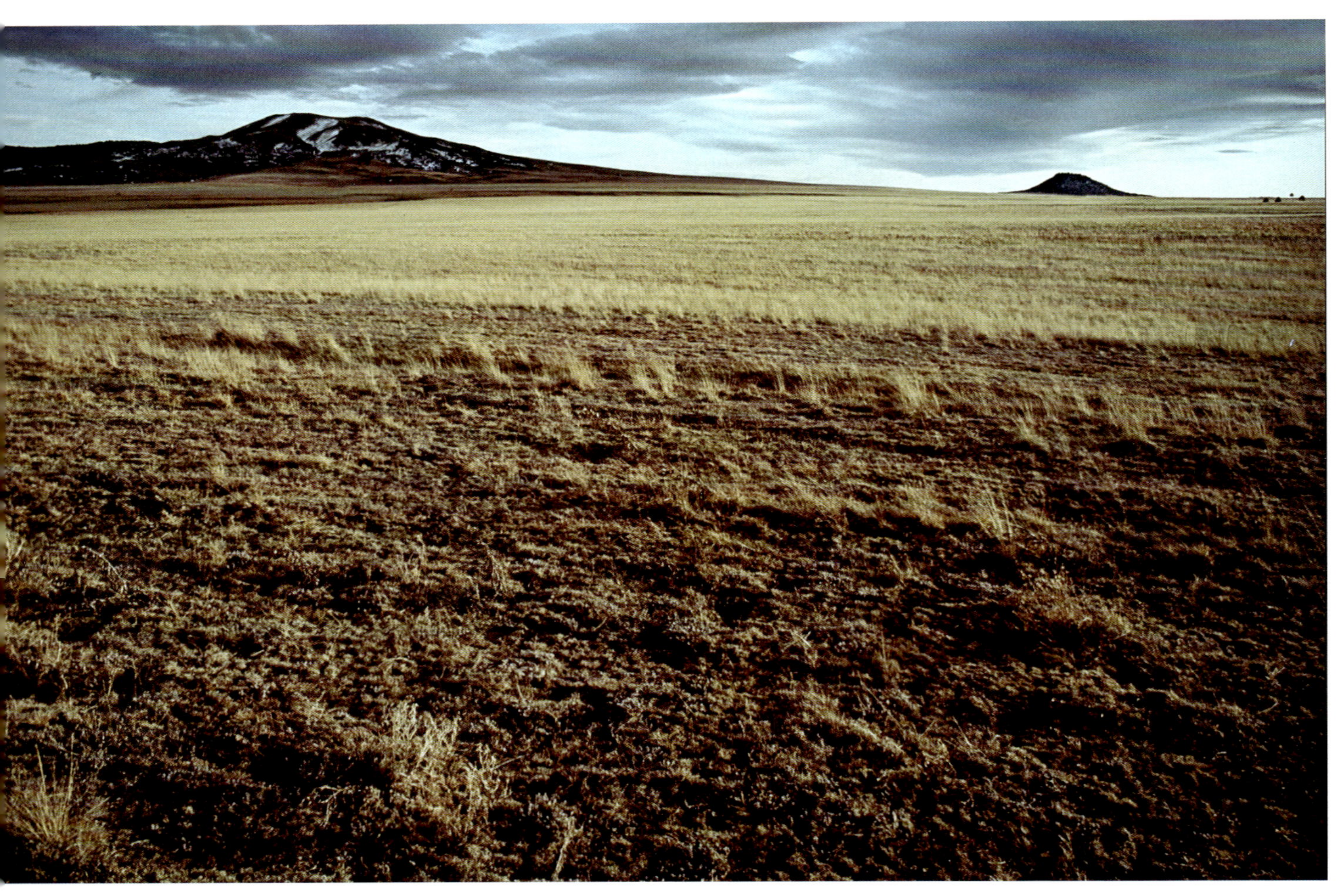

Galisteo Basin.

Joan Brooks Baker

November

4
Monday

5
Tuesday

Election Day

6
Wednesday

7
Thursday

8
Friday

◑

9
Saturday

10
Sunday

November

S	M	T	W	T	F	S
					1	2
3	4	5	6	7	8	9
10	11	12	13	14	15	16
17	18	19	20	21	22	23
24	25	26	27	28	29	30

December

S	M	T	W	T	F	S
1	2	3	4	5	6	7
8	9	10	11	12	13	14
15	16	17	18	19	20	21
22	23	24	25	26	27	28
29	30	31				

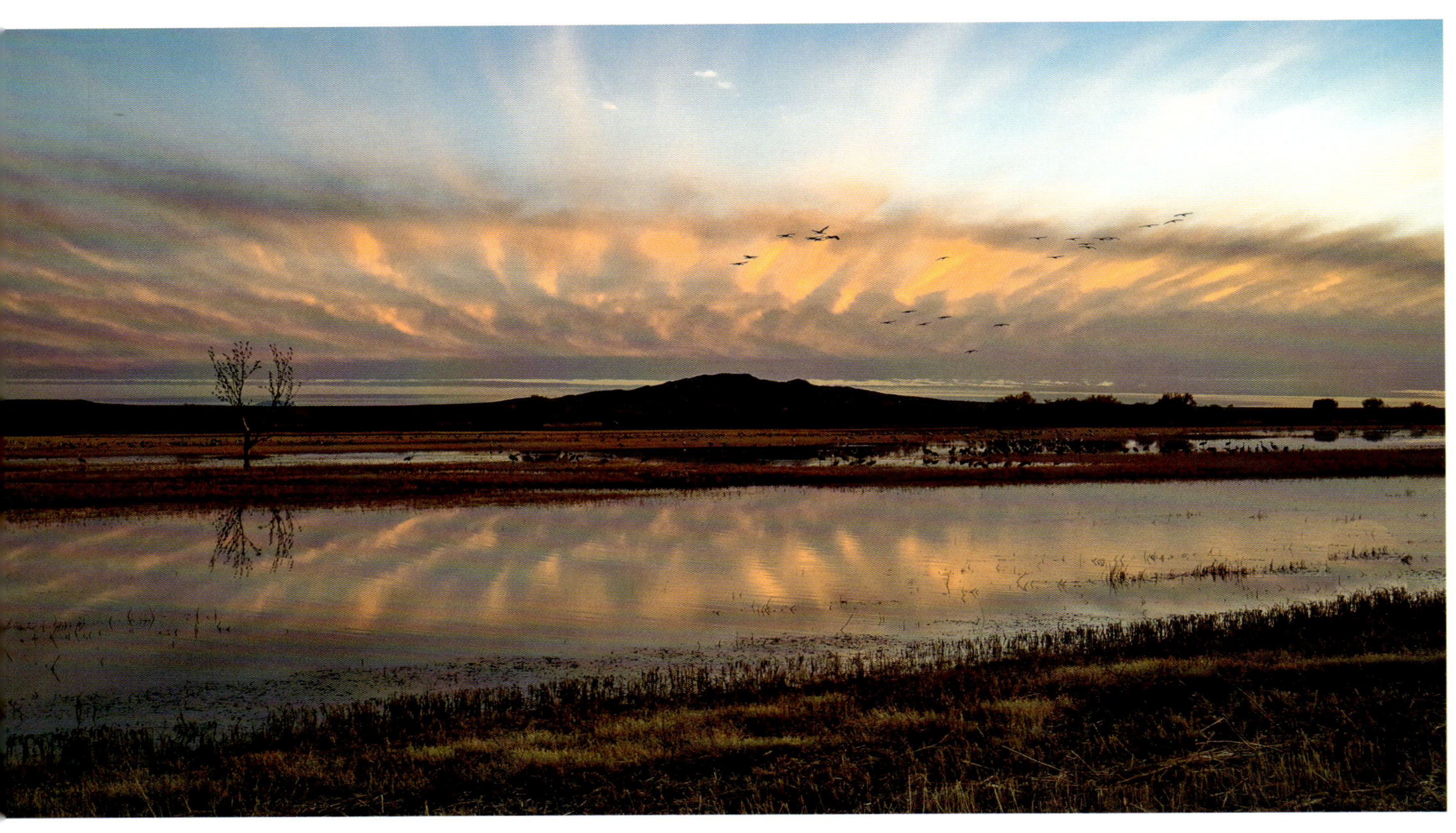

Bosque del Apache National Wildlife Refuge.

Tony Bonanno

November 11   Monday

Veterans Day, Free admission for veterans at NM state-run museums and historic sites, newmexicoculture.org

November 12   Tuesday

San Diego Feast Day with various dances at Jemez and Tesuque Pueblos, indianpueblo.org/feast-days/

November

11
Monday

Veterans Day

12
Tuesday

13
Wednesday

14
Thursday

15
Friday

16
Saturday

17
Sunday

November

S	M	T	W	T	F	S
					1	2
3	4	5	6	7	8	9
10	11	12	13	14	15	16
17	18	19	20	21	22	23
24	25	26	27	28	29	30

December

S	M	T	W	T	F	S
1	2	3	4	5	6	7
8	9	10	11	12	13	14
15	16	17	18	19	20	21
22	23	24	25	26	27	28
29	30	31				

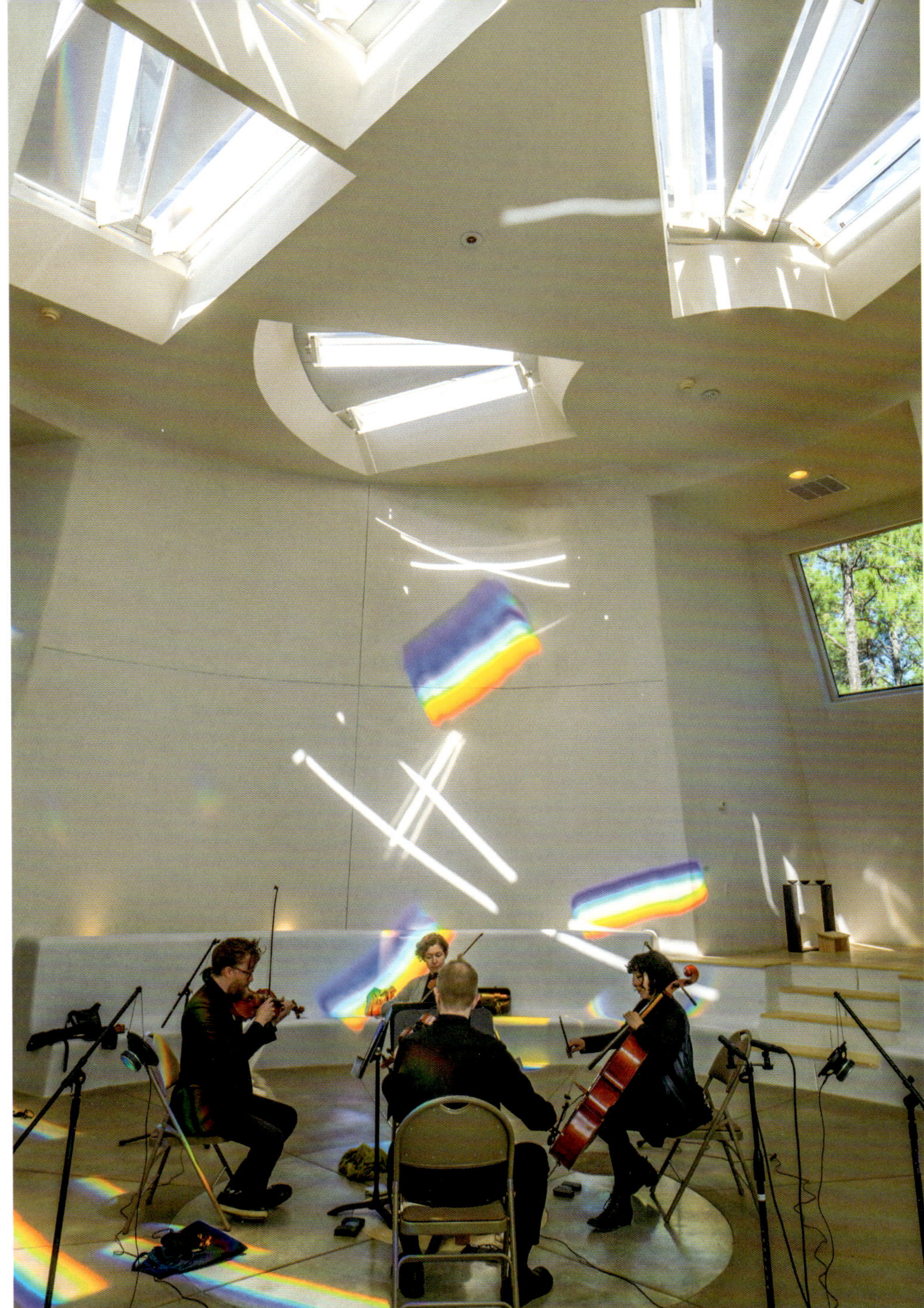

Musicians warm up prior to a private concert in the Dwan Light Sanctuary on the United World College campus near Las Vegas.

Kitty Leaken

November 23   Saturday

Las Cruces International Mariachi Conference, lascrucesmariachi.org (through November 26)

November

18
Monday

19
Tuesday

20
Wednesday

21
Thursday

22
Friday

23
Saturday

24
Sunday

November

S	M	T	W	T	F	S
					1	2
3	4	5	6	7	8	9
10	11	12	13	14	15	16
17	18	19	20	21	22	23
24	25	26	27	28	29	30

December

S	M	T	W	T	F	S
1	2	3	4	5	6	7
8	9	10	11	12	13	14
15	16	17	18	19	20	21
22	23	24	25	26	27	28
29	30	31				

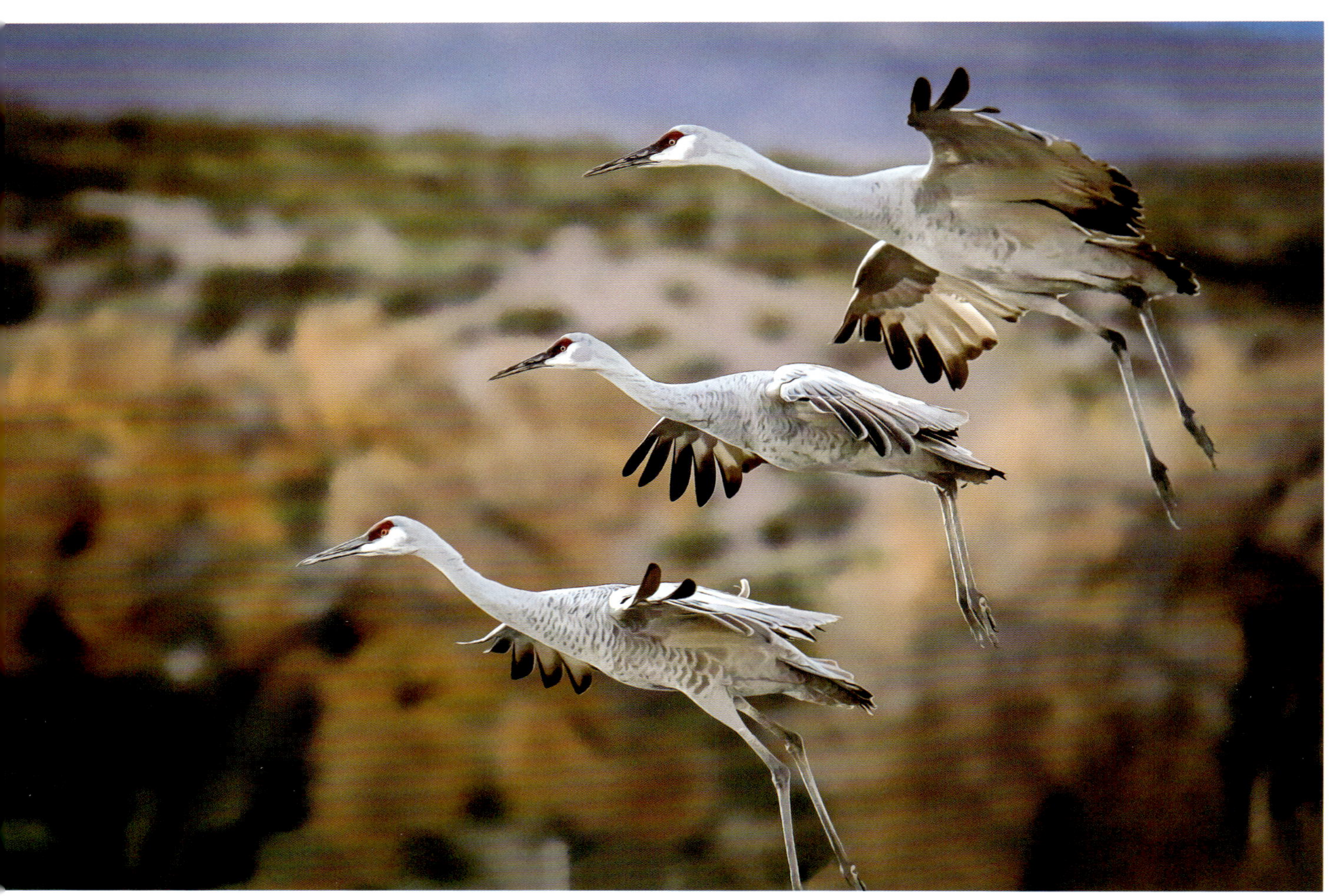

At twilight, a family of sandhill cranes descends on a
roosting pond at the Bosque del Apache National Wildlife
Refuge during the annual Festival of Cranes celebration.

Kim Ashley

Christmas on the Pecos, Pecos River in Carlsbad, christmasonthepecos.com (through December 31, no rides on December 24)

November

25
Monday

26
Tuesday

27
Wednesday

28
Thursday

Thanksgiving Day

29
Friday

Native American Heritage Day

30
Saturday

●

December

1
Sunday

World AIDS Day
First Sunday of Advent

November

S	M	T	W	T	F	S
					1	2
3	4	5	6	7	8	9
10	11	12	13	14	15	16
17	18	19	20	21	22	23
24	25	26	27	28	29	30

December

S	M	T	W	T	F	S
1	2	3	4	5	6	7
8	9	10	11	12	13	14
15	16	17	18	19	20	21
22	23	24	25	26	27	28
29	30	31				

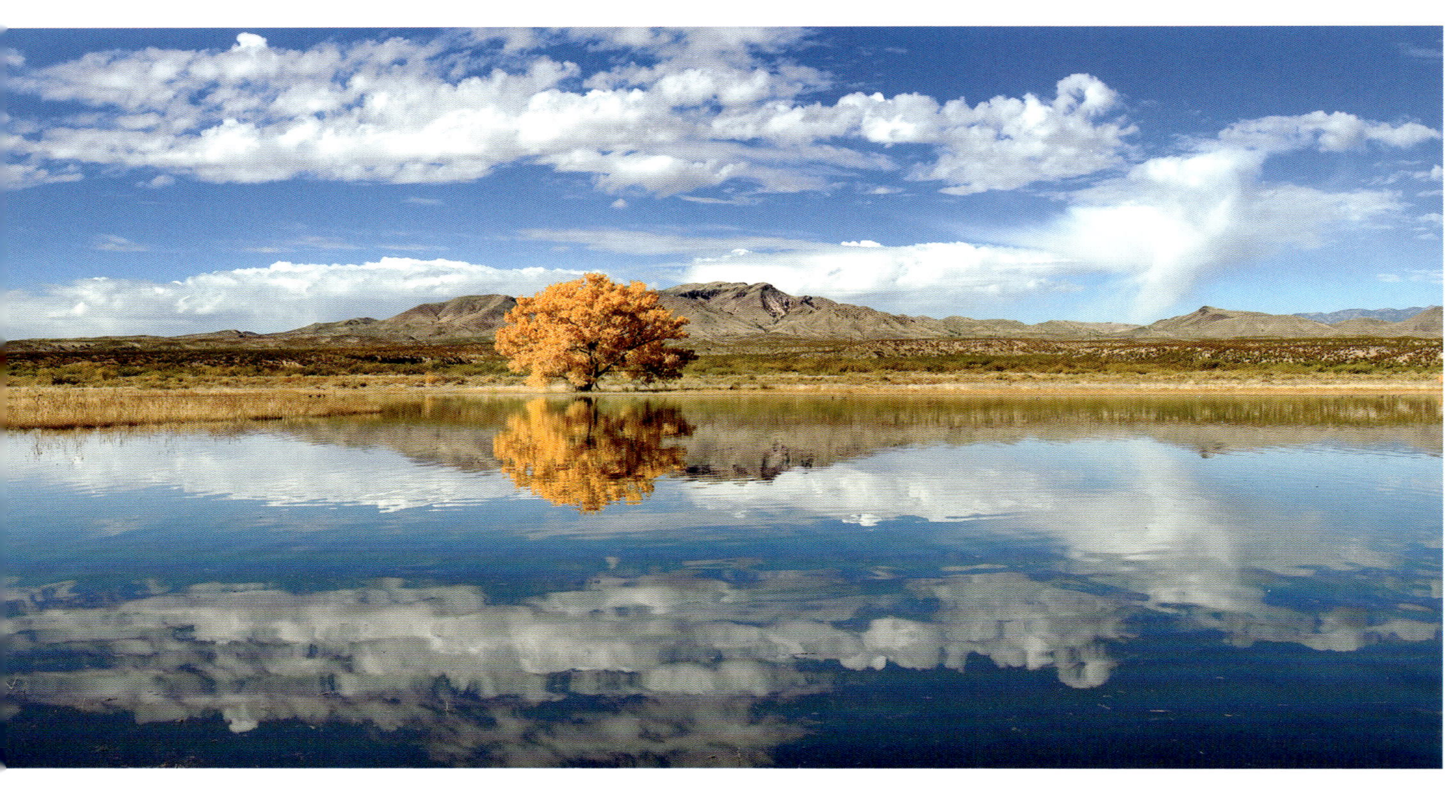

Bosque del Apache
National Wildlife Refuge.

Geraint Smith

Festival of the Cranes, Bosque del Apache National Wildlife Refuge, friendsofthebosquedelapache.org (through December 8)

December

2
Monday

3
Tuesday

National Cookie Day

4
Wednesday

5
Thursday

6
Friday

Pearl Harbor Remembrance Day (1941)

7
Saturday

◑

8
Sunday

December

S	M	T	W	T	F	S
1	2	3	4	5	6	7
8	9	10	11	12	13	14
15	16	17	18	19	20	21
22	23	24	25	26	27	28
29	30	31				

January 2025

S	M	T	W	T	F	S
			1	2	3	4
5	6	7	8	9	10	11
12	13	14	15	16	17	18
19	20	21	22	23	24	25
26	27	28	29	30	31	

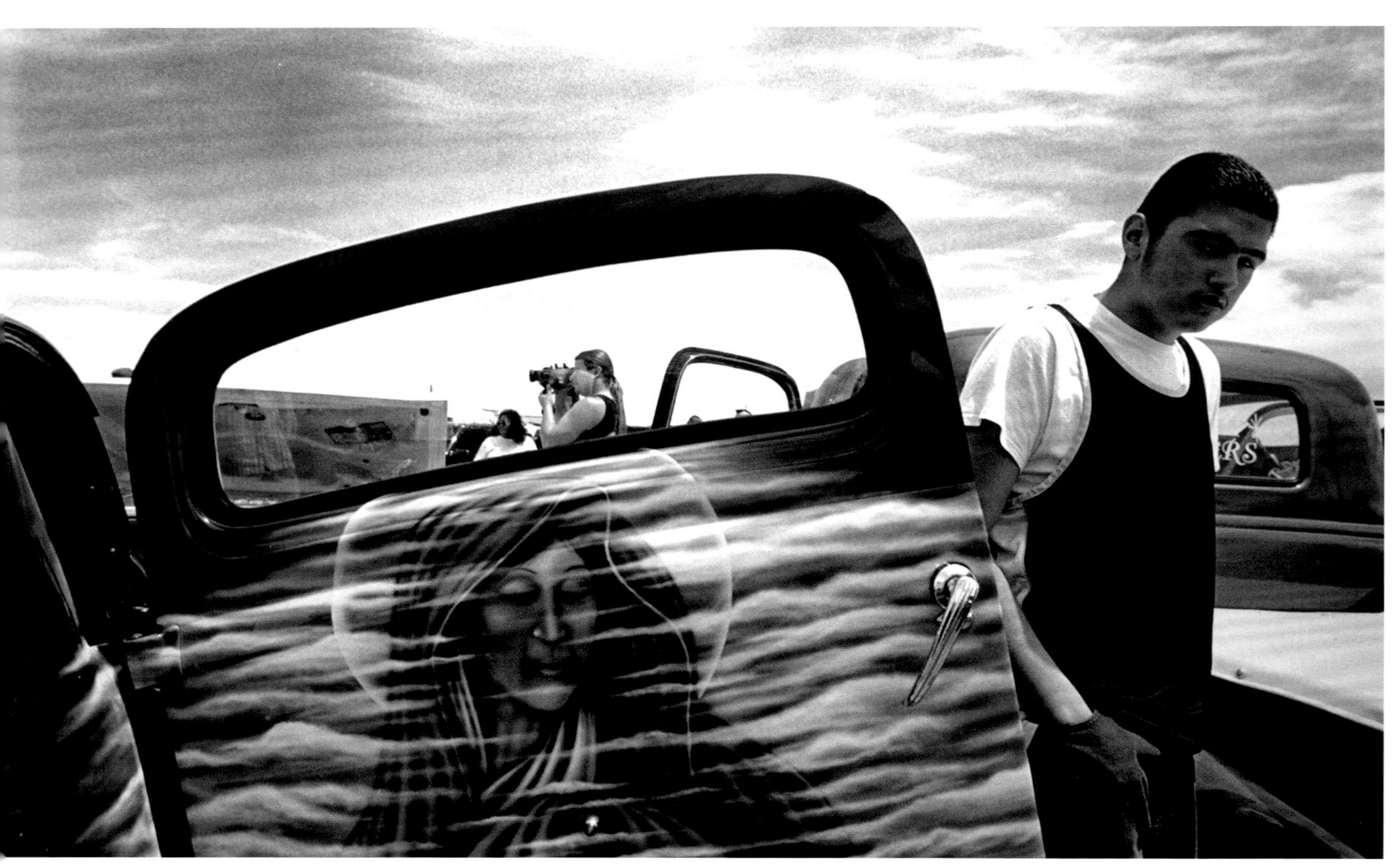

At a lowrider car show in Española. Courtesy of the Palace of
the Governors Photo Archives, Sam Adams Collection.

Sam Adams

Nuestra Señora de Guadalupe Feast Day with mass and dances at Pueblo of Pojaque, pojaque.org; Matachines Dances at Pueblo of Jemez, jemezpueblo.com

December

9
Monday

10
Tuesday

11
Wednesday

12
Thursday

Feast of Our Lady of Guadalupe

13
Friday

14
Saturday

15
Sunday

Bill of Rights Day
○

December

S	M	T	W	T	F	S
1	2	3	4	5	6	7
8	9	10	11	12	13	14
15	16	17	18	19	20	21
22	23	24	25	26	27	28
29	30	31				

January 2025

S	M	T	W	T	F	S
			1	2	3	4
5	6	7	8	9	10	11
12	13	14	15	16	17	18
19	20	21	22	23	24	25
26	27	28	29	30	31	

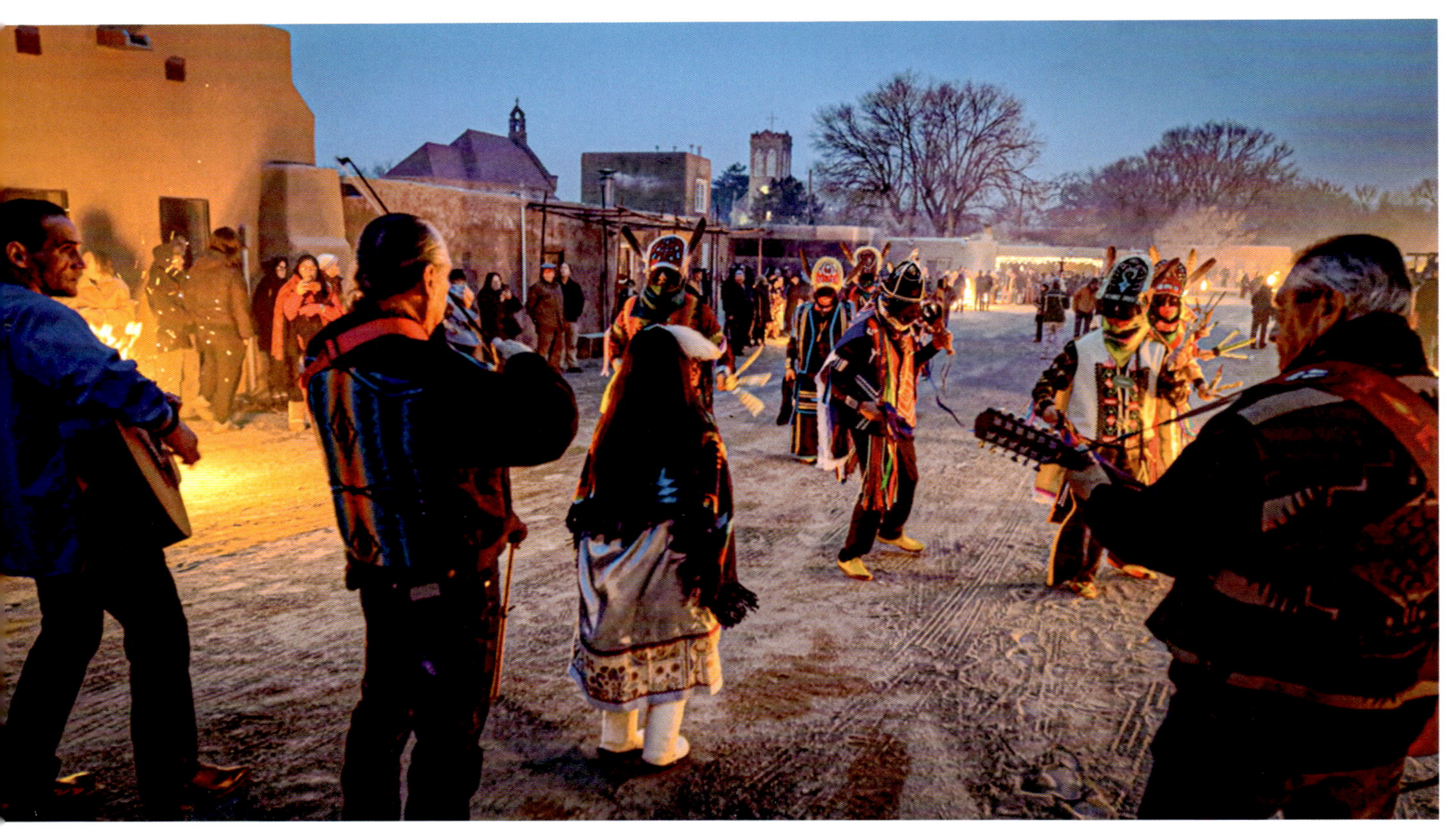

A community procession and Los Matachines dancers on Christmas Eve at the San Juan Bautista Church at Ohkay Owingeh Pueblo.

Robert Brewer

December

16 Monday

17 Tuesday

18 Wednesday

19 Thursday

20 Friday

December

S	M	T	W	T	F	S
1	2	3	4	5	6	7
8	9	10	11	12	13	14
15	16	17	18	19	20	21
22	23	24	25	26	27	28
29	30	31				

January 2025

S	M	T	W	T	F	S
			1	2	3	4
5	6	7	8	9	10	11
12	13	14	15	16	17	18
19	20	21	22	23	24	25
26	27	28	29	30	31	

Winter Solstice

21 Saturday

◑

22 Sunday

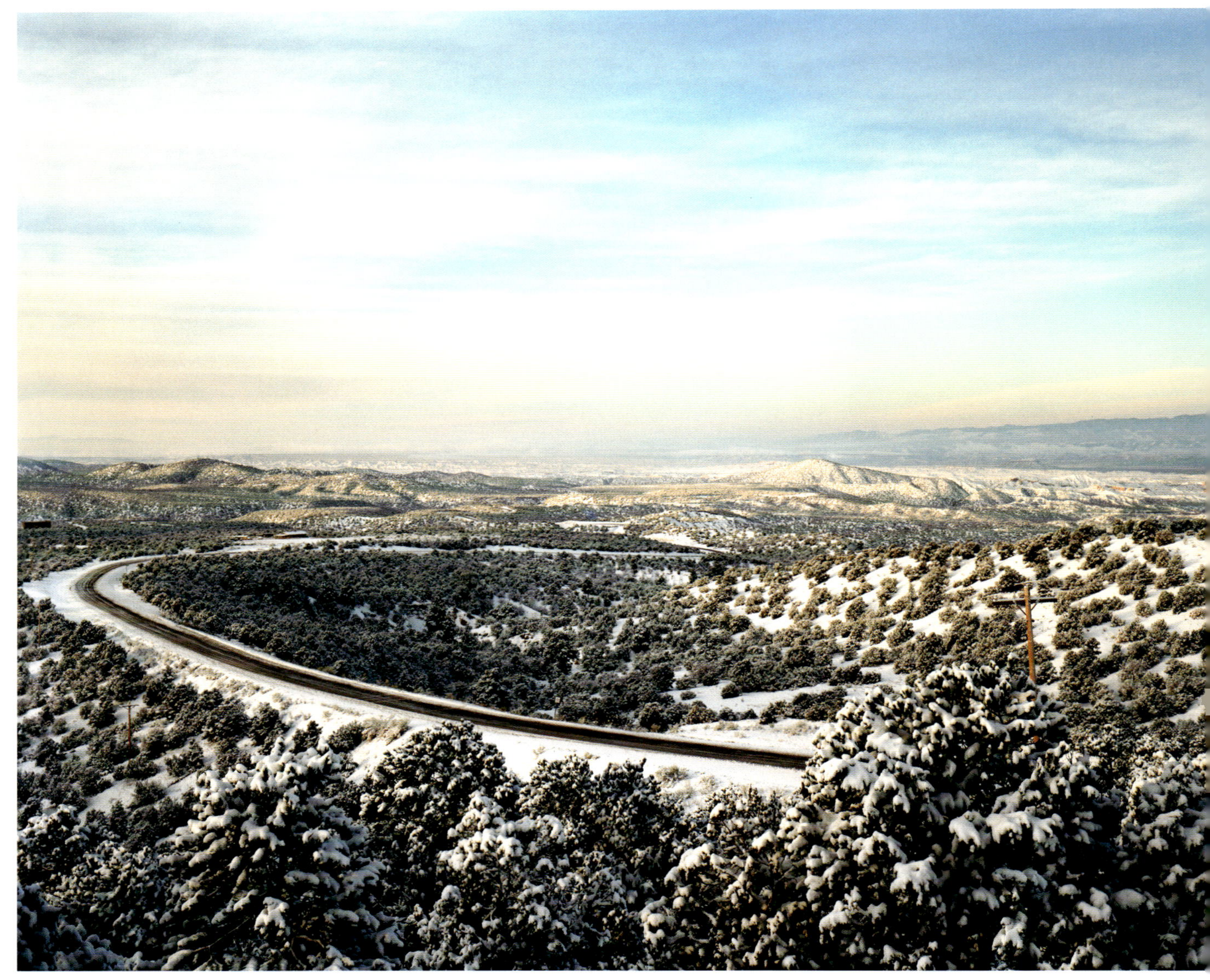

The High Road above Cordova.

Alex Harris

December

S	M	T	W	T	F	S
1	2	3	4	5	6	7
8	9	10	11	12	13	14
15	16	17	18	19	20	21
22	23	24	25	26	27	28
29	30	31				

January 2025

S	M	T	W	T	F	S
			1	2	3	4
5	6	7	8	9	10	11
12	13	14	15	16	17	18
19	20	21	22	23	24	25
26	27	28	29	30	31	

23
Monday

24
Tuesday

Christmas Eve

25
Wednesday

Christmas Day
Hanukkah (begins sundown December 25 and ends nightfall January 2, 2025)

26
Thursday

Kwanzaa (ends on January 1, 2025)

27
Friday

28
Saturday

29
Sunday

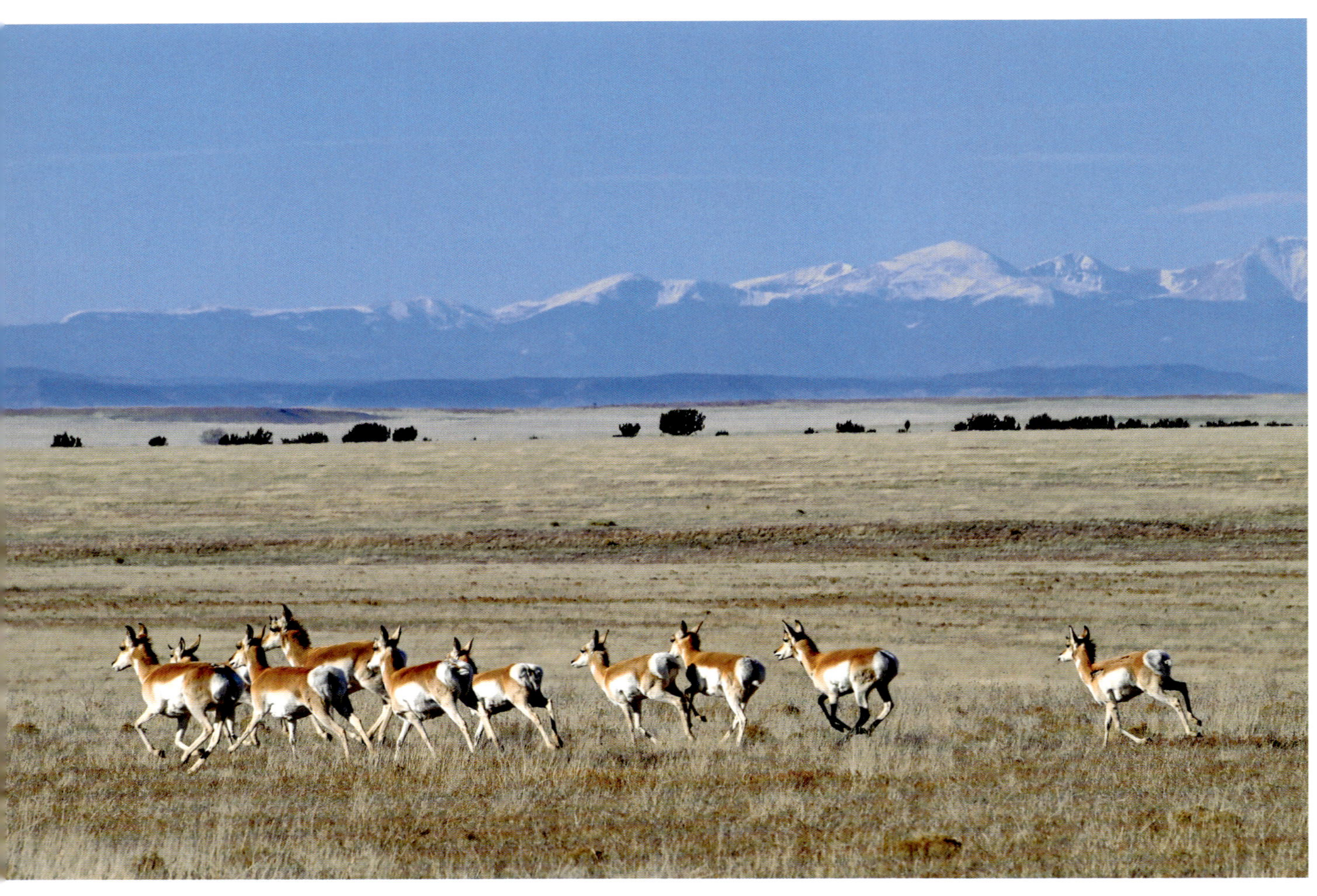

Pronghorn antelope, Kiowa National
Grassland in Harding County.

Gene Peach

December

30
Monday

●

31
Tuesday

New Year's Eve

January

1
Wednesday

New Year's Day

2
Thursday

3
Friday

4
Saturday

5
Sunday

December

S	M	T	W	T	F	S
1	2	3	4	5	6	7
8	9	10	11	12	13	14
15	16	17	18	19	20	21
22	23	24	25	26	27	28
29	30	31				

January 2025

S	M	T	W	T	F	S
			1	2	3	4
5	6	7	8	9	10	11
12	13	14	15	16	17	18
19	20	21	22	23	24	25
26	27	28	29	30	31	

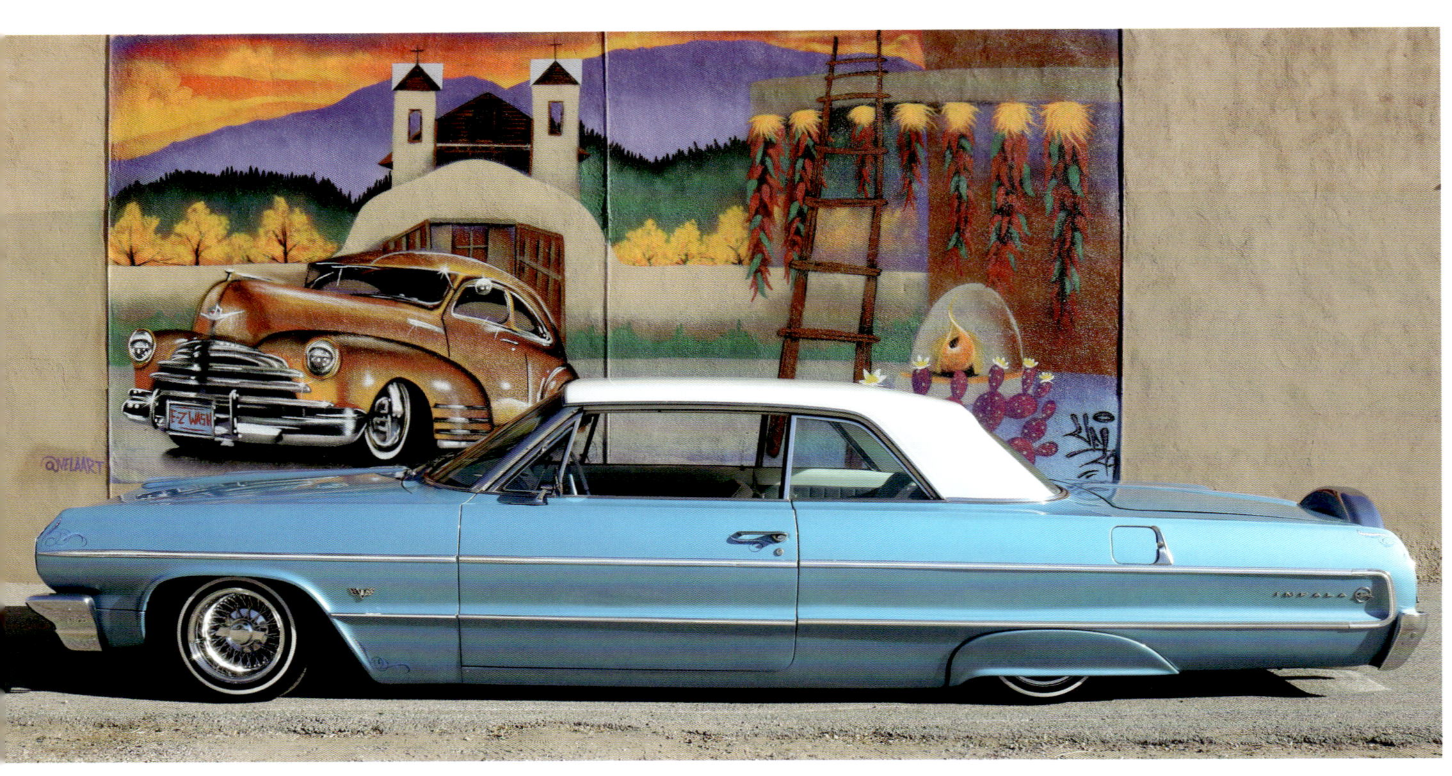

This beautiful 1964 Impala belongs to Charles Vigil
of Chimayó. Photo was taken in Española at E-Z Way
Laundry, and the background mural was done by Vela Art.

Aaron Anaya

The Photographers

Sam Adams (1927–2022) was a retired motion picture and television literary agent who moved to Santa Fe in 1989. In 2005, he won the New Mexico Council on Photography's Eliot Porter Award. His work has been exhibited at the Chimayó History Museum, Center for Contemporary Art, Palace of the Governors, University of New Mexico, El Museo Cultural, and the University of Oklahoma. Choosing film over digital media, he produced thousands of black-and-white pictures captured around the world. He jealously guarded his amateur status and remained deeply rooted in the in the twentieth rather than the twenty-first century. His archive is held by the Palace of the Governors Photo Archives and is one of the first collections in the Photo Legacy Project.

Aaron Anaya is a lowrider/Chicano artist from the small town of Alcalde in the heart of northern New Mexico. His main focus is to keep the traditions and spirit of the area—such as lowriders, the Catholic faith, and Hispano culture—alive for generations to come through his photography, poetry, and in-depth storytelling. Anaya is well-known for photographing lowrider vehicles, their owners, and old churches. Instagram: @AaronAnaya72; Facebook: @Aaron Anthony Anaya

Jim Arndt is a nationally recognized advertising and editorial photographer who specializes in location productions and environmental portraiture. He is the recipient of more than five hundred photography and advertising awards, was named *Adweek National Photographer of the Year*, and was one of American Photographer's top photographers. His work has been exhibited in galleries in Minneapolis, Austin, Taos, Santa Fe, and Paris. His photography is in the permanent collection of the Museum of New Mexico. He has taught at the Minneapolis College of Art and Design and the Santa Fe Photographic Workshops. Arndt's publications include *How to Be a Cowboy*, *The Cowboy Boot Book*, *Art of the Boot*, *100 Years of Western Wear*, *Cowboy Boots*, *Art of the Cross*, *Art of Turquoise*, *Buckaroo Boots*, and his Cowboy Boot calendars. He lives in Santa Fe. jimarndtphotography.com

Kim Ashley is a retired professional photographer and teacher living in Albuquerque. While in the army, he worked as a darkroom technician and photojournalist. He is the author of three books, including a travel guide, *Photographing Albuquerque*. His acclaimed portraits of Hopi, Navajo, and Pueblo Indian children were exhibited at the Governor's Gallery in Santa Fe.

Joan Brooks Baker has been a photographer almost since childhood. She began photographing on New York City's streets with her school's shoebox camera in order to catch her surrounding chaos. Baker has shown her images at galleries in Santa Fe, New York, and in a most meaningful exhibit at the United Nations, *60 Women from 50 Countries*. Her several-years-long project on the Black Madonna resulted in an oral/photographic presentation shown in the US and Europe, a project that led her to write her memoir, *The Magnolia Code*, which received the 2020 Independent Press Distinguished Favorite Award for Memoir and was a finalist for the 2020 Arizona/New Mexico Book Awards in the "Memoir" category.

Evalyn Bemis has lived in Santa Fe for more than thirty years. Her passions are photography, horses, and conserving wild places. Of her photography, she says, "I make photographs daily. I see things through my lens that might otherwise be unnoticed. Sometimes I go in search of images; sometimes they are right under my nose. I often leave the comforts of what I know. I accept uncertainty as my companion and trust my intuition. . . . If I can capture and share one thing, it is that beauty and joy can be found everywhere. It is our choice to see it."

Tony Bonanno is a professional photographer based in Santa Fe. His subjects have ranged from the President and First Lady of the United States to Indigenous peoples and their cultures, to capturing the beauty and rhythms of running horses. Fine art prints from his *White Horses of the Camargue*, *CubaStreet*, *Synergy*, and *Hooves & Dust* portfolios are in numerous collections both in the US and abroad.

The Photographers

Robert Brewer's enchantment with photographing New Mexico started the 1970s, and his work on faith, culture, and architecture culminated in *The Persistence of Memory: New Mexico's Churches*. It received regional and national awards as well as New Mexico Museum and traveling exhibitions. Photographic collaborations at Los Alamos resulted in books on the Cerro Grande fire and *Science in the National Interest*. His website is lightningstrikestwice.net.

Taos photographer Steven Bundy has been documenting the American Southwest for more than two decades. His work is represented by Tularosa Basin Gallery of Photography in Carrizozo; Panterra Gallery in Bisbee, AZ; and the Blumenschein Museum in Taos. His images are included in the permanent collections of the State of New Mexico's Art in Public Places program; the Albuquerque Museum's permanent art collection; the Gus Foster Collection at the Harwood Museum in Taos; the International Photography Hall of Fame and Museum permanent collection; and in numerous private collections.

Esha Chiocchio is a photographer and filmmaker who uses her combined knowledge of visual storytelling and sustainable communities to inspire social change. As an optimistic realist, she is focused on solutions to social and environmental challenges. Her current project, *Good Earth*, celebrates agrarians from diverse sectors who are revitalizing our unraveling landscapes through regenerative practices. She has photographed for commercial clients, non-profits, and magazines and has taught photography to adults and socioeconomically diverse high school students around the world. Her website is eshaphoto.com.

Bill Curry lives in northern New Mexico, where the light is magical, the cultures are potent, the people are authentic, and the creative opportunities are open-ended. His love of travel and photography has taken him to the Maldives, Jamaica, Morocco, Brazil, China, Bora Bora, Cuba, Costa Rica, Mexico, Borneo, and Australia. Yet it is the American Southwest that has captured his heart's eye with its many gifted artists, poets, painters, cowboys, and living Pueblo history. The red chile, the evening sunsets, and the smell of spring sage around Taos is fairly close to Bill's idea of living in paradise.

David Cushman is an amateur photographer who delights in photographing New Mexico's magnificent natural and cultural landscapes. David has shown his work at the Annual New Mexico Photographic Arts Show, the Albuquerque Photographers Gallery, and the Tularosa Basin Photography Gallery. He was awarded the grand prize for the 2018 *New Mexico Magazine* Photo Contest. David lives in Rio Rancho.

Emma Eckert is a visual artist and documentarian. She grew up exploring the arroyos and the dusty red sandstone bluffs of northern New Mexico. Much of her work is nature or editorial-style photography; she also enjoys making abstract and composite imagery. She lives with her husband and two children on their urban homestead in Albuquerque. See more of her work at emmaecho.com.

Bob Filice is a Santa Fe-based freelance photographer specializing in environmental portraiture, landscape, and nature. He has participated in numerous Santa Fe Photographic Workshops and in photographic journeys with the Wild Spots Foundation promoting ecotourism in Malaysia, the United Arab Emirates, Chile, Peru, and Ecuador. His images have won awards from the Photographic Society of America and have appeared in publications including *New Mexico Magazine*, *Hemispheres*, *New Mexico Outdoors*, *Solar Today*, *Modern Adobe in New Mexico*, *Santa Fean* magazine, and *American Indian Review*.

William Frej, an award-winning photographer, has created three recent photography books. *Maya Ruins Revisited: In the Footsteps of Teobert Maler* (Peyton Wright Press, 2020), has received fourteen awards, including five separate Best Photography Book of the Year awards. His second book, *Seasons of Ceremonies: Rites and Rituals in Guatemala and Mexico* (Museum of New Mexico Press, 2021), has won twelve awards, including four Photography Book of the Year awards. A third book, *Travels

Across the Roof of the World: A Himalayan Memoir, with Anne Frej, was published by George F. Thompson Press (2022). *Blurred Boundaries*, on rock art in the Southwest, with Polly Schaafsma, will be published by the Museum of New Mexico Press in 2023.

Kirk Gittings has resided in New Mexico for sixty-three years. He studied photography at the University of New Mexico and later received his MA in photography from the University of Calgary in Alberta, Canada. His work has been widely published and exhibited and is held in permanent collections in the United States, Canada, and Europe. He has taught photography at the University of New Mexico, the School of the Art Institute of Chicago, and the Santa Fe University of Art and Design. Gittings has led numerous workshops and has received many honors and awards, including the University of New Mexico's distinguished alumnus Zia Award.

Theodore Greer was born in Gallup, where his parents and grandparents ran trading posts on the Navajo and Zuni Indian reservations. He studied photography and printmaking at San Francisco Art Institute and at the University of New Mexico. Greer's images have been exhibited in Jemez Springs, Santa Fe, Taos, Albuquerque, Phoenix, Flagstaff, Seattle, Oakland, and San Francisco and appear in many publications, including *New Mexico Magazine*. Hundreds of his photographic canvases have been purchased for display by the Presbyterian Hospital system around the state, providing a soothing, hopeful environment for patients, visitors, and healthcare providers alike. He lives in Jemez Springs with his wife Donna Lea, a fabric artist. His work can also be seen at the Jemez Artisans Gallery in Jemez Springs, Walatowa Visitor Center in Jemez Pueblo, Tularosa Basin Gallery of Photography in Carrizozo, and Rust Medical Center in Rio Rancho. His website is www.theodoregreer.com.

David Halpern, a resident of Santa Fe, was born in Nashville, TN, attended the University of Missouri, and earned a degree from Vanderbilt University. He has led photography workshops and taught photography on the university level. He's had more than fifty solo exhibitions in museums and galleries throughout the country and served thirteen times as a National Parks artist-in-residence. A prolific writer, he has published books and received awards for two editions of *Tulsa Art Deco*. His photographs are included in the archives of the National Park Service and several public and private collections, and in 2004 he was inducted into the Tulsa Historical Society's Hall of Fame. More than eight hundred images of America's national parks by Halpern recently became part of the archives of the National Park Service History Collection at Harpers Ferry, West Virginia. His website is davidhalpern.com.

Alex Harris taught photography for four decades at Duke University, where he is a founder of the Center for Documentary Studies. He photographed extensively in New Mexico during the 1970s and 1980s, publishing several books on the region including *Red White Blue and God Bless You: A Portrait of Northern New Mexico*. His work is represented in major collections at museums including The San Francisco Museum of Modern Art, the J. Paul Getty Museum in Los Angeles, and the High Museum of Art in Atlanta. His awards include a Guggenheim Fellowship in Photography, a Rockefeller Foundation Humanities Fellowship, and a Lyndhurst Prize.

Tom Quinn Kumpf is an internationally recognized, award-winning photographer, writer, poet, and storyteller whose work has appeared in publications and exhibitions throughout the US, Europe, and the former Soviet Union. He is author of eleven books including the award-winning *Children of Belfast, Ireland: Standing Stones to Stormont* and *Two Sides: Haiku and Other Words*. He works primarily in documentary, fine art, travel, and portrait photography, and he teaches individual and group photo workshops. He operates a studio and is a year-round resident of Taos, and he is available to interested parties by appointment.

Kitty Leaken moved to New Mexico after graduating from Stanford University with a degree in history. She grew up overseas to parents in the diplomatic service, and her interests in culture and anthropology that brought her to

The Photographers

Santa Fe have guided her work around Tibetan immigrants, Sri Lankan orphans, and Native American artists. She learned photojournalism on the job at the *Santa Fe Reporter* and the *Santa Fe New Mexican*. Her photographs of a community of Tibetans in Santa Fe were featured in an award-winning special section in the *Santa Fe New Mexican*, in an exhibit at the Museum of International Folk Art, and in the book *Art of Exile: Paintings by Tibetan Children in India* (MNMP). Leaken photographed Native American communities for *Contemporary Native American Artists* and *Kevin Red Star: Crow Indian Artist* (both Gibbs Smith). Her photos have also appeared in several cookbooks. Most recently, her portraits were featured in the exhibit *Honoring Tradition and Innovation: 100 Years of Santa Fe's Indian Market* at the New Mexico History Museum. Her website is kittyleaken.com.

Judy McGowan is a retired land use and community planner and a photographer with an interest in western history and the landscape, both natural and as touched by long interaction with people. Covid isolation pushed her interest in exploring the world of night sky photography. Her photographs have been included in group shows in Santa Fe and Albuquerque and solo exhibits in Telluride, Colorado.

Daniel Nadelbach and **Gilda Meyer-Niehof** have been working together internationally in the photography business for more than thirty years in various capacities from photography and videography; production and art direction; fashion and architectural styling; hair and makeup; and model agency ownership. Clients include Auberge Resorts, Western Interiors & Design, One & Only Resorts, Whole Foods, CGH Earth India, HEAD Sportswear, St. Regis Hotels and Resorts, Sotheby's, and Tago Tulum. Gilda's interior design and jewelry design work can be seen on Instagram @jadudesigns. Daniel's website is www.nadelbachphoto.com and he is on Facebook and Instagram @danielnadelbachphoto. Daniel is also an FAA Certified/Licensed UAS Drone Pilot, which allows him to meet addition photography and videography needs of his clients.

Steve Northup grew up in Santa Fe and has been a professional photographer for about fifty years, working as a staff photographer for United Press International in the San Francisco, Miami, and Saigon bureaus, later going on to work for the *Washington Post* and *TIME* magazine. He was awarded a Nieman Fellowship at Harvard University. He spent fourteen years as the photographer for the Santa Fe Living Treasures program and was named a Living Treasure in 2019. His picture archives are at the Briscoe Center for History at the University of Texas in Austin. He and his wife, Martha, live in Santa Fe.

After years of working in fashion and design in San Francisco, Milan, Paris, and New York, photographer **Peter Ogilvie** surrendered to the call of the wild and, in 2004, relocated both his home and studio to Santa Fe. "There is nothing quite like the open spaces of New Mexico. Though my travels have taken me all over the planet to beautiful places both urban and wild, I have come to deeply savor the vast skies and landscape of the Southwest. It is all about the light. It verges on the surreal and continually surprises me."

Gene Peach has been photographing the cultures and landscapes of New Mexico for more than thirty years. His work appears regularly in magazines and books and has been featured on more than three hundred publication covers. Peach is author and photographer of the award-winning books *Making a Hand: Growing Up Cowboy in New Mexico* and *Santa Fe* (both MNMP); and photographer for *Los Luceros: New Mexico's Morning Star* (MNMP) and *Santa Fe Icons: 50 Symbols of the City Different* (Rowman & Littlefield). He is currently creating a book project titled *Devoción: Historic Churches of Northern New Mexico*. He lives in Santa Fe. His website is genepeach.com.

Geraint Smith is a landscape, nature, and wildlife photographer living in San Cristobal, a village nestled in the Sangre de Cristo Mountains of northern New Mexico. Geraint has spent forty-five years traveling and photographing the land, architecture, and people of the Southwest. He is respected as a fine art photographer and leading expert photo guide. He offers personalized photography workshops with instruction in all aspects of photography in New Mexico, Colorado, and the Four Corners region of the American Southwest. His work has appeared in national and international publications. His fine art prints are hanging in countries all over the world. He is the author of the book *Rio Grande del Norte: An Intimate Portrait* (MNMP, 2019).

Zubin Stillings is a photographer, writer, and cinematographer from Santa Fe. Growing up with professional photographer parents, he learned photography from a young age. He used this background as a jumping-off point to join the media, film, and TV worlds. After finishing up a gap year, Zubin will be attending Emerson College in the fall of 2023 as he continues to work as a photographer and TV screenwriter.

Scott Swearingen has had a love for and an active pursuit of the photographic medium since his teens. He continues to enjoy learning new digital and alternative techniques from his home in Santa Fe.

Bill Todino has been photographing, exhibiting, and selling his photography in New Mexico since 2006. The blend of cultures, incredible colors of the Southwest, and fantastic New Mexico skies are mostly the photographic subjects for Bill. Primarily a landscape photographer, he is comfortable in color and black and white, enjoys street photography, detail work, and the quirky nature of urban and rural settings. Bill is essentially self-taught, enhancing his craft with professional workshops, domestic and international. He has exhibited in several galleries and community art spaces in New Mexico. His website is billtodino.zenfolio.com.

Cassandra Trevino, a native of Santa Fe, is a full-time cyber security professional who uses photography as her peaceful getaway. Her photography, focusing on native birds, other animals, and beautiful landscapes is a part-time hobby. This hobby takes her to some of the most beautiful places in New Mexico. Cassandra's photography has been featured in the *New Mexico Treasures Engagement Calendar* for a few years. One of the roadrunners that Trevino photographed is featured on a New Mexico license plate through the Share with Wildlife program. See more of Cassandra's work here: fb.me/RoadrunnerGirlWildlifePhotography.

Don J. Usner grew up in Los Alamos and Chimayó. He has published photographs in several books that he wrote or co-authored, including *Sabino's Map: Life in Chimayó's Old Plaza*, *Valles Caldera: A New Vision for New Mexico's National Preserve*, and *Oralé! Lowrider: Custom Made in New Mexico* (all MNMP), as well as *Chasing Dichos Through Chimayó* (UNM Press). He has also written and provided photographs for numerous magazines and online publications and worked as a photojournalist for Searchlight New Mexico. His website is donusner.com.

Brian VanDenzen is an amateur photographer and attorney living in Santa Fe. As a child, he explored the lakes, prairies, and forests of his native Wisconsin. He first traveled to New Mexico as a teen, using his camera's viewfinder to discover the landscape, light, and culture of the Land of Enchantment. After moving here in 2002 to practice law, the camera became his creative voice to share the beauty of New Mexico's environment, history, and people. His images have been published in *Outdoor Photographer Magazine* and *New Mexico Magazine* and displayed in galleries across the state. His website is DesertDogPhotography.com.

Jane Whitmore, a clinical psychologist and former archeologist, has lived in New Mexico for forty-eight years. In 2018, she closed her clinical psychology practice to focus on her photography and writing projects with the goal of promoting human rights, respect for cultural diversity, and compassion for the human condition. In 2021 she received the CENTER Project Launch grant for The Bikini Project. She was awarded a Santa Fe

Photographic Workshops scholarship, had two solo exhibits of her *Enduring Traditions* project, and participated twice in two-person exhibits of *Española: People and Places*. Find more at JaneWhitmorePhotography.com and TheBikiniProject.org.

Fred Wilbur fell in love with New Mexico after coming to Taos in the early 1970s for archaeology field school. He has owned galleries in holography, art glass, and photography in Dallas, Santa Fe, Fort Worth, Atlanta, and southern Colorado. After retiring, he returned to New Mexico and has continued his lifelong hobby of taking landscape and nature photographs. Some of his photographs are currently on display in the El Potrero Trading Post in Chimayó and Chimayó Rocks in Española. His website is Fredwilburphotography.com.

Bob Young is a freelance writer and photographer focusing on the landscape and ancient cultures of the Southwest. He has been a contributor to *New Mexico Magazine*, with feature articles on the Salinas Pueblos of the Estancia Basin and Hispanic homesteads of Largo Canyon in northwestern New Mexico. His images have appeared in numerous magazines, calendars, books, and exhibitions. His recently published book, *Images of Dinetah*, with archaeologist James Copeland, is available from bobyoungphoto@msn.com. A retired physician, Young lived in Farmington for more than eighteen years before relocating to Naples, Florida. Find more at Rockartfineart.com.

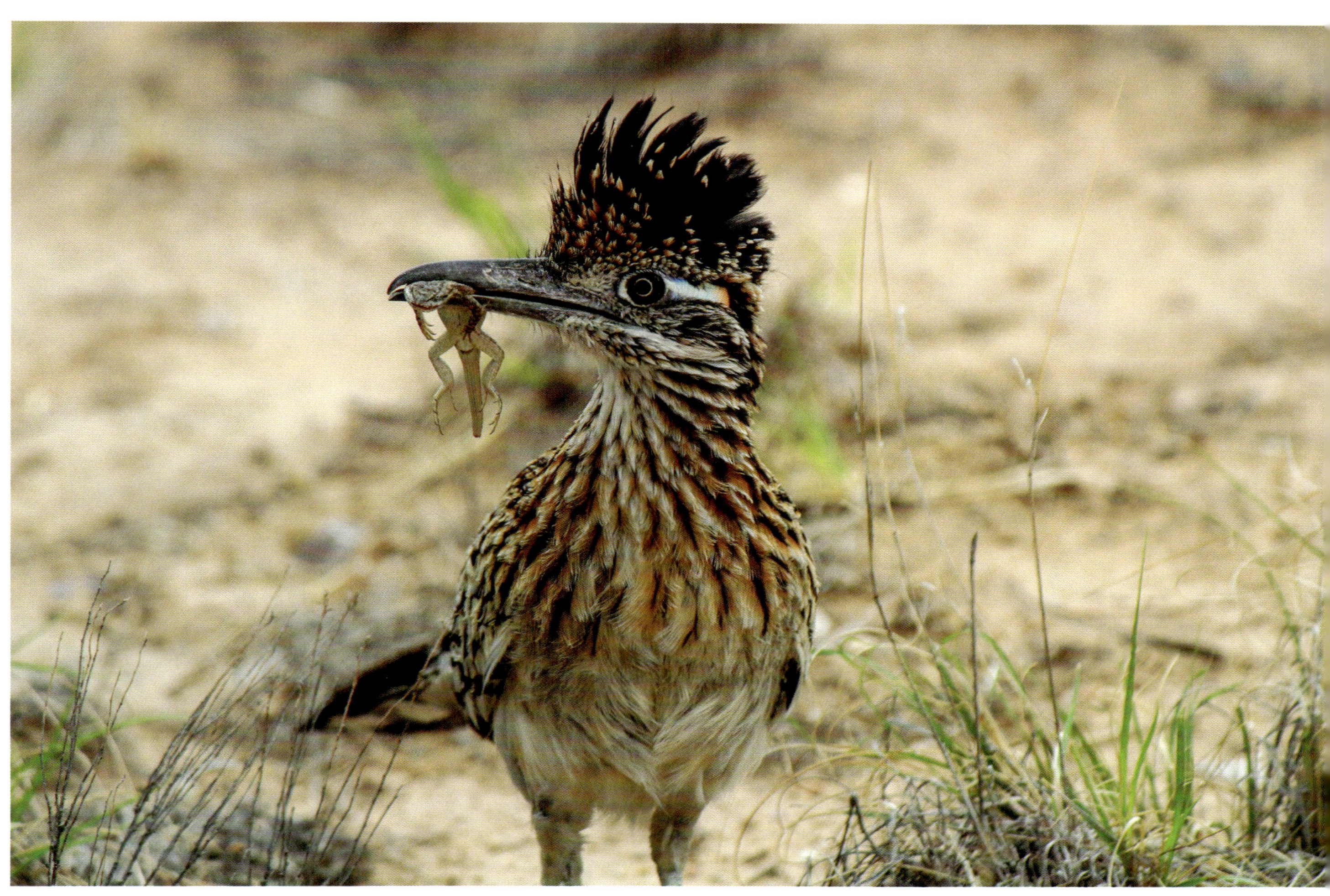

Roadrunner with lunch on the run in Albuquerque.

Cassandra Trevino

2024

January						
S	**M**	**T**	**W**	**T**	**F**	**S**
	1	2	3	4	5	6
7	8	9	10	11	12	13
14	15	16	17	18	19	20
21	22	23	24	25	26	27
28	29	30	31			

February						
S	**M**	**T**	**W**	**T**	**F**	**S**
				1	2	3
4	5	6	7	8	9	10
11	12	13	14	15	16	17
18	19	20	21	22	23	24
25	26	27	28	29		

March						
S	**M**	**T**	**W**	**T**	**F**	**S**
					1	2
3	4	5	6	7	8	9
10	11	12	13	14	15	16
17	18	19	20	21	22	23
24	25	26	27	28	29	30
31						

April						
S	**M**	**T**	**W**	**T**	**F**	**S**
	1	2	3	4	5	6
7	8	9	10	11	12	13
14	15	16	17	18	19	20
21	22	23	24	25	26	27
28	29	30				

May						
S	**M**	**T**	**W**	**T**	**F**	**S**
			1	2	3	4
5	6	7	8	9	10	11
12	13	14	15	16	17	18
19	20	21	22	23	24	25
26	27	28	29	30	31	

June						
S	**M**	**T**	**W**	**T**	**F**	**S**
						1
2	3	4	5	6	7	8
9	10	11	12	13	14	15
16	17	18	19	20	21	22
23	24	25	26	27	28	29
30						

July						
S	**M**	**T**	**W**	**T**	**F**	**S**
	1	2	3	4	5	6
7	8	9	10	11	12	13
14	15	16	17	18	19	20
21	22	23	24	25	26	27
28	29	30	31			

August						
S	**M**	**T**	**W**	**T**	**F**	**S**
				1	2	3
4	5	6	7	8	9	10
11	12	13	14	15	16	17
18	19	20	21	22	23	24
25	26	27	28	29	30	31

September						
S	**M**	**T**	**W**	**T**	**F**	**S**
1	2	3	4	5	6	7
8	9	10	11	12	13	14
15	16	17	18	19	20	21
22	23	24	25	26	27	28
29	30					

October						
S	**M**	**T**	**W**	**T**	**F**	**S**
		1	2	3	4	5
6	7	8	9	10	11	12
13	14	15	16	17	18	19
20	21	22	23	24	25	26
27	28	29	30	31		

November						
S	**M**	**T**	**W**	**T**	**F**	**S**
				1	2	3
4	5	6	7	8	9	10
11	12	13	14	15	16	17
18	19	20	21	22	23	24
25	26	27	28	29	30	

December						
S	**M**	**T**	**W**	**T**	**F**	**S**
1	2	3	4	5	6	7
8	9	10	11	12	13	14
15	16	17	18	19	20	21
22	23	24	25	26	27	28
29	30	31				

2025

January

S	M	T	W	T	F	S
			1	2	3	4
5	6	7	8	9	10	11
12	13	14	15	16	17	18
19	20	21	22	23	24	25
26	27	28	29	30	31	

February

S	M	T	W	T	F	S
						1
2	3	4	5	6	7	8
9	10	11	12	13	14	15
16	17	18	19	20	21	22
23	24	25	26	27	28	

March

S	M	T	W	T	F	S
						1
2	3	4	5	6	7	8
9	10	11	12	13	14	15
16	17	18	19	20	21	22
23	24	25	26	27	28	29
30	31					

April

S	M	T	W	T	F	S
		1	2	3	4	5
6	7	8	9	10	11	12
13	14	15	16	17	18	19
20	21	22	23	24	25	26
27	28	29	30			

May

S	M	T	W	T	F	S
				1	2	3
4	5	6	7	8	9	10
11	12	13	14	15	16	17
18	19	20	21	22	23	24
25	26	27	28	29	30	31

June

S	M	T	W	T	F	S
1	2	3	4	5	6	7
8	9	10	11	12	13	14
15	16	17	18	19	20	21
22	23	24	25	26	27	28
29	30					

July

S	M	T	W	T	F	S
		1	2	3	4	5
6	7	8	9	10	11	12
13	14	15	16	17	18	19
20	21	22	23	24	25	26
27	28	29	30	31		

August

S	M	T	W	T	F	S
					1	2
3	4	5	6	7	8	9
10	11	12	13	14	15	16
17	18	19	20	21	22	23
24	25	26	27	28	29	30
31						

September

S	M	T	W	T	F	S
	1	2	3	4	5	6
7	8	9	10	11	12	13
14	15	16	17	18	19	20
21	22	23	24	25	26	27
28	29	30				

October

S	M	T	W	T	F	S
			1	2	3	4
5	6	7	8	9	10	11
12	13	14	15	16	17	18
19	20	21	22	23	24	25
26	27	28	29	30	31	

November

S	M	T	W	T	F	S
						1
2	3	4	5	6	7	8
9	10	11	12	13	14	15
16	17	18	19	20	21	22
23	24	25	26	27	28	29
30						

December

S	M	T	W	T	F	S
	1	2	3	4	5	6
7	8	9	10	11	12	13
14	15	16	17	18	19	20
21	22	23	24	25	26	27
28	29	30	31			

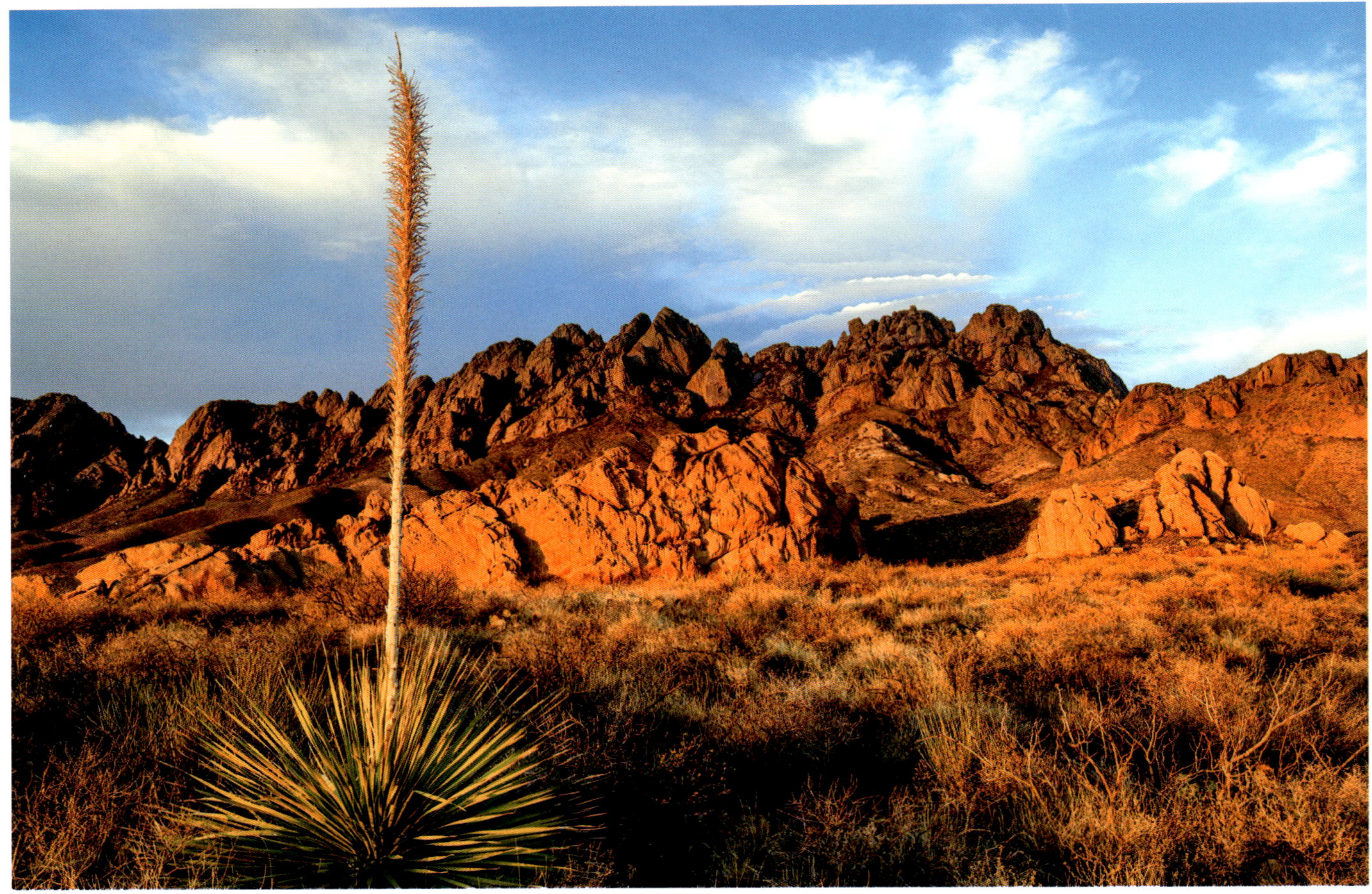

Above: Desert spoon cactus at sunset, Dripping Springs Natural Area, Organ Mountains-Desert Peaks National Monument, Doña Ana County. Photograph by Brian VanDenzen.

Cover: Bosque del Apache National Wildlife Refuge. Photograph by Tony Bonanno.

Pages 2–3: Raven in flight over White Sands. Photograph by Daniel Nadelbach/Gilda Meyer-Niehof .

Special event dates are liable to change. Please check with event organizers directly for the most up-to-date information.

Manufactured in Canada.

ISBN 978-0-89013-680-5

Museum of New Mexico Press
PO Box 2087
Santa Fe, New Mexico 87504
mnmpress.org